Don Green

W9-CDS-443

Preventing Silent Heart Disease

Also by Harold L. Karpman, M.D.
Your Second Life

Preventing Silent Heart Disease

Detecting and Preventing
America's Number 1 Killer

HAROLD L. KARPMAN, M.D., F.A.C.C., F.A.C.P.

Foreword by H. J. C. Swan, M.D., Ph.D., M.A.C.P.

CROWN PUBLISHERS, INC.
NEW YORK

This book is not intended as a substitute for the medical advice of physicians. The reader should regularly consult his doctor in matters relating to health and particularly in respect to symptoms that may require diagnosis or medical attention.

Published by Crown Publishers, Inc., 201 East 50th Street, New York, New York 10022

CROWN is a trademark of Crown Publishers, Inc.
Manufactured in the United States of America
Library of Congress Cataloging-in-Publication Data
Karpman, Harold L.
    Preventing silent heart disease / Harold L. Karpman.
        p.   cm.
    Includes index.
    1. Silent myocardial ischemia—Popular works.   I.   Title.
RC685.S48K37   1989
616.1'23—dc19

ISBN 0-517-57300-8

10 9 8 7 6 5 4 3 2 1

First Edition

To my wife, Molinda, for her
encouragement, support, and
creative contributions.

Contents

Acknowledgments

My literary agent, Ed Victor, was particularly helpful in offering editorial suggestions and, most important, in encouraging me to write the entire text by myself. This would have been impossible without the heroic efforts and skills of my editor, Jim Wade of Crown Publishers. My daughter, Laura Karpman, functioned admirably in an editorial capacity, offering suggestions and critiques even as she encouraged and motivated. My executive secretary, Caralyn Poskin, contributed in her usual dedicated and organized fashion and was helped by my transcriptionist, Marge Berlanger. Computer illustrator Majken Harden and artist Suzanne Merrick helped with the illustrations. Medical librarian Nina Hull provided the necessary library services support.

I also must give major credit to my wife, Molinda, who did all of the word processing through my many changes and drafts. She was patient beyond reason, productive in a timely fashion, and kept the project moving forward. This book exists because of her efforts, which I gratefully acknowledge.

Last, but never least, I want to thank my many patients. Our shared medical experiences have contributed enormously to many of my thoughts and conclusions.

Foreword

Heart attack, sudden death, a "coronary," high blood pressure, cholesterol—these are now terms in public conversation at almost every level of society. "No smoking," risk screening, "Is your number up?", exercise testing, and fitness centers are current responses of the public to the prevalence of atherosclerosis in Americans today. What should the healthy individual—or a patient with heart disease—do about the matter? Do the actions he or she may take really effect outcome?

Second in magnitude only to cancer research are the investigative efforts directed toward critical knowledge on the biology of atherosclerosis and of high blood pressure. Slow development of patchy changes in the arteries of the body start in adolescence in many individuals. But they occur in different vessels and to different degrees of severity at different times in the life of an individual. Basic research on arterial disease is providing many of the answers as to the cause of "hardening of the arteries" and the development of local obstructions in them. Of particular importance is atherosclerosis in the cerebral or in the coronary arteries because these vessels are naturally small and because the organs to which they supply blood are vital. Several known factors (and others not currently known) are involved and these may be interactive with one another. In patient populations in which inherited characteristics can be carefully identified and followed—and this is not easy in our mongrel human population—genetic predilections to premature generalized atherosclerosis of the coronary arteries are now becoming evident. Likewise the development of the obstructions in the coronary arteries is caused by a multitude of factors. Previously, the blood vessels of the body were thought of as a system of passive tubes lined by a soft membrane—the endothelium—whose sole purpose was to smooth the flow of blood through the tube itself. It is now recognized that the endothelial cell is a critical powerhouse for the good health of the vessel itself and, more important, for avoidance of harmful changes in the vessel walls—atherosclerosis. Atherosclerosis and the resulting obstruction in the vessel appears to be a consequence of repetitive ulceration of the vascular wall in which the internal lining membrane is harmed and exposes the tissue immediately beneath to the flowing blood. Thrombus, or clot, then forms and penetrates deeply into the vessel wall. Eventually healing occurs with restoration of the integrity of the lining membrane but with further obstruction of the vessel. Frequent episodes of ulceration and thrombosis will allow for the development of severe or even complete obstruction in a given vessel.

In addition to the genetic element, about which we can do little for ourselves, other factors may contribute to these changes. These include the level of blood pressure, the circulating level of blood fats, perhaps the sex hormones and other blood substances—certainly drugs such as nicotine—and a host of other factors unknown at the present time. The ulceration–thrombosis–healing process can obstruct a vessel so that the residual channel for blood flow is only 20 percent or less of its original size. This obstruction can cause myocardial ischemia—a situation in which the total amount of blood flow to a specific area of the heart muscle is less than needed for adequate function. It is this ischemia, or inadequate blood flow, that is harmful to heart muscle and not the presence of an obstruction in the blood vessels per se. The severity of obstruction in the blood vessels can be increased by formation of a partial or totally obstructed clot on a diseased area on a vessel, or due to constriction of the vessel wall which again reduces the available channel for blood flow. Severe reduction in blood flow to working muscle is harmful—causing paralysis of function, and if very severe and prolonged, death of the heart muscle itself, a "heart attack" or myocardial infarction. Thus atherogenesis is the process which initiates limitation of blood flow but it is the degree of limitation that causes transient or permanent damage to the heart muscle. It is also known that reductions in blood flow followed by a brisk restoration can cause important disturbances of heart rhythm and may cause sudden cardiac death in some people.

To the best of our knowledge, sudden unexpected cardiac death, heart attack including silent myocardial infarction (without symptoms), the acute coronary syndromes, and silent myocardial ischemia (without pain) are always associated with atherosclerotic coronary artery disease which is usually severe (greater than 80 percent narrowing of one or more major coronary vessels). The absence of coronary artery disease virtually excludes these dire complications and it is worthwhile to establish this fact. Even in patients with coronary artery disease, significant protection against premature death, stroke, or heart attack can be offered today. In the future, we look forward to limitation or elimination of atherosclerosis per se and therefore anticipate a reduction in the epidemic with which we are now faced. However, many patients will inevitably fall victim to the present scourge.

Dr. Karpman's book is intended for the informed concerned reader and is written in a manner readily understandable to the layman. It identifies several groups—the healthy but susceptible individual, the patient with known coronary artery disease, and the patient with complications of coronary artery disease such as a prior heart attack—and describes what the prudent patient in cooperation with the treating physician can do collectively to identify the presence of significant coronary disease and to minimize adverse consequences.

H. J. C. Swan, M.D., Ph.D., M.A.C.P.

1

The Ticking Time Bomb

You, a member of your family, a close friend—anyone—can be struck down without warning by a silent killer, sudden cardiac death (SCD). It kills more than 500,000 people a year, most of them needlessly. This book is designed to help you save your own life.

How Can Someone Drop Dead, Frequently Without Warning or Preexisting Symptoms?

Typically, a forty-five-year-old male, overweight, perhaps with slightly high blood pressure or mild diabetes, but otherwise in good health, relaxing and smoking a cigarette just after getting off the tennis court, or even simply sitting at his desk at nine or ten o'clock in the morning, suddenly gasps, collapses, and dies before the paramedics reach the scene. Or, less likely, he might not be overweight; he might have excellent dietary and living habits, and be hard-working and well conditioned through exercise. But it could be any one of us. We are *all* potential victims of sudden death after a certain point in our lives, unless we have taken certain reasonable and feasible precautions, and unless the right medical tests have proven that *our* particular risk of dying suddenly is minimal.

Finding the Problem

Sudden cardiac death and heart attacks are *not* inevitable; they are *always* "premature," no matter at what age they occur, and quite frequently they are preventable. Today, doctors can diagnose and treat most cardiovascular illnesses; but the biggest obstacle to achieving this goal is difficulty in getting the patient to the doctor before it's too late. Most adult heart conditions could be detected much earlier if patients formed an alliance with their cardiologists, an alliance whose major objective is to find those individuals afflicted with silent, unrecognized heart disease. This book tells you how to screen yourself and determine if you are at risk, and shows you how to use your physician to protect you against this silent killer. Such a doctor/patient partnership can delay or prevent the transition from "no heart disease" to symptomatic heart disease (i.e., angina, heart attacks) or even sudden death. This book describes the many diagnostic tools and forms of treatment that doctors have available to detect and treat silent heart disease—and can thereby help save you and thousands of others from heart attacks and sudden death. But only *you*—the reader—can do the self-screening that will get you to your doctor before it's too late. I have written this book not only to inform you, but also to persuade you to visit your doctor earlier rather than later.

You will learn about certain less common heart tests, such as Holter monitoring, that may be necessary to use along with the widely known resting electrocardiogram and the stress (or treadmill) test to determine if you are at risk and why, and you will find out what to do before and when you go to your doctor.

It is my hope that as you digest the information in this book, a positive change in your attitude will occur. That slight revision in outlook and in activities may help to preserve your health—and your life.

Who Is at Risk?

Men are at greater risk of developing silent heart disease than are women, especially if they are overweight, have high blood pressure, a clear family history of premature coronary heart disease, elevated blood cholesterol, diabetes, have a sedentary lifestyle, and/or smoke cigarettes. Other risk factors, such as emotional or physical stress, may also contribute to the early onset of coronary artery disease. All of these factors will be explored in this book. If an individual is in the "high risk" category, it is absolutely essential that he or she be screened for symptom-free heart disease, now known as *silent myocardial ischemia* (SMI). Even screening of certain "low risk" patients should also be carefully considered for a variety of reasons that will be outlined later.

What Is the Current Size and Impact of the Heart Problem in the United States?

Unfortunately, the exact answer to this question is unknown. Only recently have cardiologists recognized that the heart disease statistics published by the National Center for Health Statistics of the U.S. Public Health Service, by the American Heart Association, and by the National Heart Institute may have been grossly understated. The incredible fact is that the number of deaths from heart disease in the United States *in one year* exceeds the *combined* total of American fatalities due to AIDS (1981 to present) and injuries sustained in World Wars I and II, the Korean War, and the Vietnam War (see Figure 1).

Coronary heart problems cause more death, disability, and economic loss in industrialized nations than does any other group of illnesses. We are in the midst of an epidemic of heart disease!

The Facts

Each year, in the United States alone:

- At least 500,000 persons die suddenly.
- Approximately 1 million Americans die from diseases of the heart and blood vessels, almost as many as all other

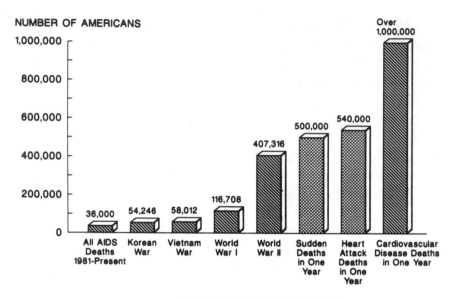

Figure 1. Comparison of cardiovascular mortality in the United States with deaths from other causes.

causes of death combined (see Figure 2). One death occurs every 32 seconds.

- About 1½ million Americans will have heart attacks, and of the 540,000 of them who die, more than 300,000 will do so before they reach the hospital (see Figure 3).
- More than 284,000 patients were subjected to coronary artery bypass surgery and 133,000 to balloon angioplasty in 1986, and the numbers are increasing each year.
- Total costs are well over $94 billion, including lost wages.

How Many People Have *Undiagnosed* Silent Myocardial Ischemia (SMI)?

The numbers are incredible. People afflicted with *diagnosed* coronary artery heart disease constitute the "tip of the iceberg," a total of 5.4 million people, but the hidden majority may be a figure two to four times greater, and even that estimate may actually be conservative.

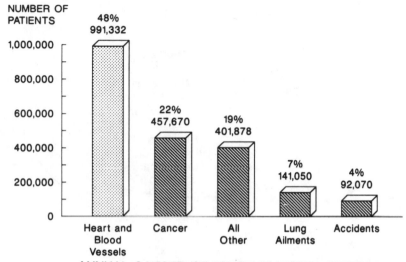

ANNUAL CAUSES OF DEATH IN UNITED STATES

Figure 2.   Cardiovascular disease causes almost 50% of all deaths in the
United States.

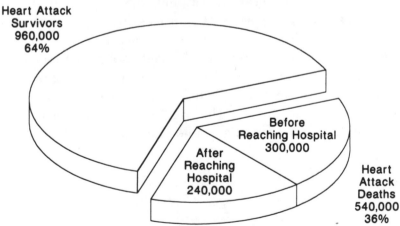

Figure 3.   The majority of heart attack deaths occur before the
victim reaches the hospital.

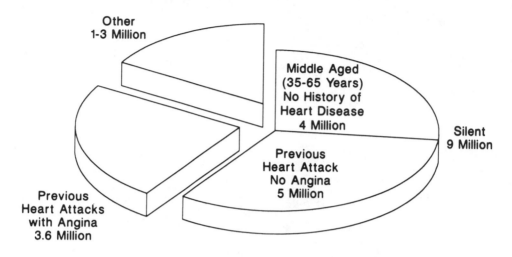

Figure 4. Estimated frequency of silent myocardial ischemia.

Between 2.5 percent and 10 percent of totally symptom-free middle-aged males (i.e., ages 35–65) are afflicted with this absolutely silent, smoldering heart problem. Adding in the 5 million patients who previously have suffered heart attacks and who may have SMI, the 3.6 million patients who have SMI associated with recurrent chest pains, middle-aged women, and the thousands (if not millions) of patients with SMI who are *not* middle-aged, brings the total to at least 12 million Americans (see Figure 4) who are carrying on their normal activities despite being afflicted with unsuspected (and therefore undetected) heart disease. The frightening fact is that it's as if each one of them were carrying a time bomb in their chests.

Silent Myocardial Ischemia

Heart attacks happen when not enough blood flows through the coronary arteries. In most instances, the flow is blocked by atherosclerosis (or arteriosclerosis), fatty deposits in the coronary arteries, which thicken and harden the arteries. This porridge-like material builds up at an extremely slow rate and eventually may completely block an affected artery (seeFigure 5); when this occurs, a heart attack usually follows. But it has become quite clear in recent years that major problems can arise even when the arteries are only minimally or moderately narrowed by the atherosclerosis.

Oxygen starvation of the heart is the most important cause of angina, death of heart tissue (i.e., "heart attacks"), malfunctions of heart rhythms (i.e., palpitations or "skipping" of the heart), and sudden death. Completely silent (i.e., painless) episodes of heart oxygen starvation may occur anytime, even at the beginning of the atherosclerotic process, when the fatty material is just beginning to be deposited in the coronary arteries, and even though significant blockages have not yet developed. This condition is called *silent myocardial ischemia* (SMI), a painless and therefore usually undetected transient decrease of coronary artery blood supply, which may last for only a few seconds or may last for many minutes or even hours.

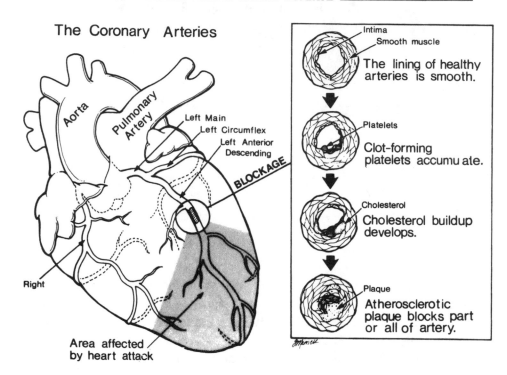

Figure 5.   Anatomy of the coronary arteries and illustration of how a cholesterol
plaque builds up and blocks an artery.

The Dynamic Coronary Artery

For obvious reasons, in past years cardiologists and pathologists have focused only on atherosclerotic blockage of the coronary arteries as the principal cause of heart attacks, malfunctions of heart rhythms, and/or sudden death. In fact, obstruction of the blood flow in the coronary artery by fatty deposits was, and still is, considered the most important single cause of these events. But scientific evidence is forcing doctors to look beyond the concept of simple narrowing or blockage of a coronary artery to that of a more dynamic and complex process that is responsible for most coronary heart problems.

Both silent and painful coronary heart problems are caused by narrowing or complete blockage of the coronary arteries resulting from various combinations and permutations of intermittently *active* narrowing (i.e., vasoconstriction or spasm) of the muscular coronary artery wall that occurs in regions of *fixed* (i.e., rigid narrowing or blockage) arteriosclerotic plaquing. In other words, if the lumen (passageway) of a coronary artery has been narrowed to, say, 70 percent of its normal size by a cholesterol plaque, it may be yet further narrowed (or completely closed) by spasm of the arterial wall itself or by an unpredictable and intermittently increased tendency for rapidly flowing blood to clot in certain key locations (see Figure 6).

Although episodes of ischemia (poor coronary artery blood flow) are totally symptom-free (no pain or other warning sensations) in at least three out of four instances, they are detectable even in these very early stages by relatively simple tests. Early discovery of ischemia, especially in the symptom-free individual, is terribly important, since the victim may never know that he or she is afflicted with heart disease until he or she actually experiences an acute heart attack or heart failure. Sudden death may be the *first* sign of a heart problem in many unfortunate cases. Because physicians, in the past, have relied primarily upon angina (chest pain) to alert them to the onset of significant coronary heart disease, the *true* onset of meaningful heart disease has frequently not been detected during the smoldering days, weeks, or years prior to the onset of symptoms or to the occurrence of sudden death.

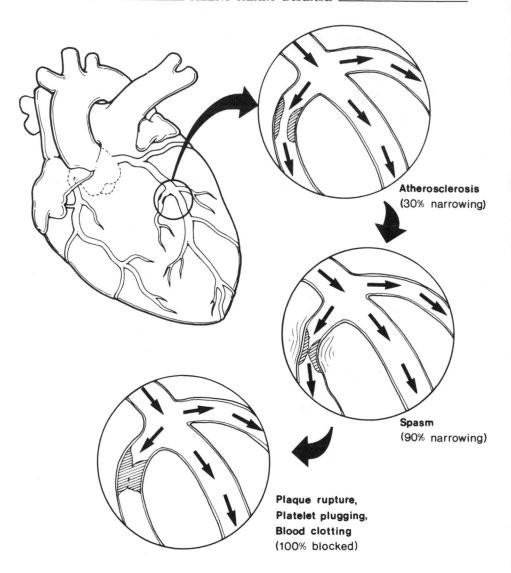

Figure 6.   Coronary artery can become blocked when effects of spasm are added to narrowing produced by atherosclerotic plaque, cholesterol buildup, and blood clotting.

Causes of SMI

Supply and Demand

The amount of blood pumped from the heart at any time depends on the body's needs at that moment. More blood is required if one is exercising, experiencing anxiety or stress, or taking certain drugs. These activities cause the heart to beat faster and, as a consequence, the heart itself requires more blood delivered through the coronary arteries to nourish the heart muscle. The amount of blood being delivered through abnormally narrowed or diseased arteries may be more than adequate to supply the needs of a heart beating at a slow or resting rate if the body's requirements are relatively minimal, such as when sleeping or resting. But if the body's blood-flow requirements are increased (as in exercise), the heart rate speeds up and the heart demands more blood flow through the coronary arteries. If the narrowed coronary arteries can't deliver enough blood, a significant heart reaction (e.g., SMI, angina, heart attack, sudden death, etc.) will occur.

Surprisingly, most episodes of ischemia, whether painful or not, are *not* brought on by increases in the heart rate. In fact, the heart rates associated with most episodes of SMI that occur during ordinary daily activity are usually significantly lower than the rates observed in the same patients who develop SMI while on a treadmill, when the heart rate is much higher because of the effects of exercise.

Spasm in the muscular layer of the coronary artery wall frequently causes SMI even in patients with only minimal arteriosclerotic lesions (e.g., when the artery is narrowed only by 20 to 30 percent). These occurrences are particularly ominous since they can happen quite suddenly and without warning, in diseased or *even in perfectly normal* arteries and, often, when the heart rate is slow or normal and *not* when it is fast. Therefore, SMI may not be triggered by the increased heart rate which occurs during the course of a diagnostic stress test (treadmill test), whereas it might be detected by Holter monitoring (see Chapter 10) which records the electrocardiogram at all times, whether the heart rate is slow or fast, and during times when coronary artery spasm might be happening.

To summarize, most episodes of SMI probably result from transient *decreases* in coronary artery blood flow rather than from *increases* in oxygen need such as those precipitated by the increased heart rates produced by exercise, emotion, drugs, or other factors. A *combination* of decreased blood flow and increased oxygen demand is almost certainly present in every patient with SMI. The concept of chest pain caused by a fast heart rate as the only warning sign of heart disease is therefore totally incorrect, since most episodes of SMI, inadequate blood flow to the heart, are not painful and are not caused or triggered by an increased heart rate.

Timing of SMI

Circadian Rhythm

The sequence of occurrence, magnitude, and duration of episodes of SMI is, at the present time, totally unpredictable for the individual patient, but certain key patterns are starting to emerge. SMI may be prolonged (60 minutes or longer) or brief (from 30 to 60 seconds) and may or may not be associated with chest pain. Chest pain develops during the course or at the *end* of only approximately 25 percent of SMI episodes—it is rarely present at the *beginning*.

In 1983, Drs. John Deanfield and Andrew Selwyn and their colleagues in London clearly demonstrated that the greatest frequency of both painful and pain-free episodes of SMI took place in the morning, between 6:00 A.M. and noon. When this data was analyzed for "time of awakening," the early-morning increase of SMI episodes was striking. More episodes took place in the first and second hour after arising, at a time when patients are least likely to be exerting themselves and their heart rates are usually quite slow. The episodes of SMI were generally found to follow a 24-hour, biological time sequence known as a *circadian rhythm pattern*.

Although heart attacks have been found to be randomly distributed throughout the months of the year and the days of the week, their onsets tend to follow the same circadian pattern as SMI, occurring more frequently from 6:00 A.M. to noon, with the maximum number between 9:00 and 10:00 A.M. It is interesting to note that these findings are consistent for *all* classifications of patients, whether old or young, men or women, smoker or nonsmokers, coffee drinkers or nondrinkers or whether or not they had a previous history of anginal chest pains or heart attacks.

Causes of SMI and Heart Attacks

We know that approximately 90 percent of all heart attacks are caused by an *arteriosclerotic nodule* or *plaque,* frequently ruptured or spontaneously broken up, resulting in blockage of the coronary artery. It should be clear, however, that heart attacks do not occur simply because of the plaque rupture itself, but instead are contributed to by the enlargement of the blood *thrombus* (or clot) that forms around the plaque (usually following rupture) and blocks the flow of blood through the coronary artery. (See Figure 5.)

Clotting occurs because of a tendency for blood elements known as *platelets* to clump together, quite possibly because of an increased production of the "stress hormones" *adrenaline* and *noradrenaline* (epinephrine and norepinephrine) manufactured by one of the body's special nervous systems, the sympathetic nervous system. Other factors may also be important in facilitating blood clotting, but platelet clumping appears to be the main cause. Simple aspirin is the best drug we have to prevent platelet clumping, and it is now being widely used to prevent and treat heart attacks.

Plaque rupture and associated blood clotting are considered the most important trigger mechanisms of heart attacks, but a host of other physiological mechanisms may also come into play, usually in the early-morning hours. First, during this time period there is frequently a blood pressure surge of 20 to 30 mm of mercury, which may increase the likelihood of plaque rupture. Next, the muscular tension in the walls of the coronary arteries may increase; if this transient increase in muscle tone is superimposed on a previously existing critical narrowing of the artery, further narrowing, decreased blood flow, and a greater probability of a complete blockage of the artery occurs. A combination of these events and possibly others that have not yet been identified appears to be responsible for the clear-cut fact that SMI, heart attacks, and sudden death tend to occur more frequently during the morning hours from 6:00 A.M. to noon, especially within the first two hours after awakening. As will be discussed in Chapter 11, this information has proven to be of extraordinary value in designing a preventative program to avoid these events.

Coronary artery spasm severe enough to cause SMI, an acute heart attack, or sudden death is a complex and dynamic process that may occur even when the fixed arteriosclerotic narrowings in the coronary artery are relatively "minor." These events may happen especially if, at the very moment of artery spasm, there is an increased demand for more coronary artery blood flow because of a rapid heart rate in response to exercise, stress, and/or drugs.

Dynamic responses such as constriction (and therefore narrowing) of the coronary artery occur in seconds, thrombosis or clotting occurs in minutes, and development of atherosclerotic lesions requires many months or years. The overall process starts when we are extremely young and ends with the damaging or even fatal events that may occur over a matter of seconds when we are older.

Angina

Angina pectoris literally means "choking in the chest," not "chest pain." Even centuries ago, the initial description of chest discomfort owing to poor coronary artery blood flow was of a rather unpleasant sensation, not chest pain per se. This subjective complaint has been characterized in a virtually endless number of ways: squeezing, pressing, aching, burning, sticking, pinching, jumping, pulsing, choking, jabbing, strangling, constricting, bursting, heartburn, gas, breathlessness, fatigue, heaviness, heavy or unpleasant feeling, and so on.

It may be located at the front of the chest, under the breastplate, across the mid-chest, in the neck, cheeks, or teeth, in the forearms or fingers, in the middle of the back, under the breasts, in the shoulders, the arms, and/or even in the elbows. It may be brought on by exercise, excitement, anger, cold weather, sexual intercourse, a rich meal, a specific body motion—or even by no activity whatsoever. It can occur when a person is simply at rest or in bed at night. It usually lasts at least 30 seconds but may continue for minutes or even for hours.

Unstable Angina: Impending Heart Attack

When angina is of new onset or if it suddenly increases in intensity and duration, occurring even at rest or with only minimal exertion, or if it is associated with profuse sweating, nausea, vomiting, shortness of breath, rapid palpitations, or profound malaise, it is called *unstable angina*. This is a sign of an impending or evolving acute heart attack. It is considered to be a medical emergency; the coronary circulation is deteriorating, suddenly becoming inadequate. It must not be ignored; immediate medical attention is necessary. Time is of the essence. If a person is unable to reach a doctor for advice or instructions, he or she should immediately call for emergency help by telephone or get to the nearest hospital emergency room by any means—ambulance, taxi, or the car of a relative or friend.

Non-cardiac Causes of Chest Pain

Chest pain may result from a variety of medical problems other than coronary artery disease. Some individuals experience chest discomfort in response to anxiety and tension, similar to the headaches that many people get when subjected to unusual emotional stress and strain. Chest pains may originate in the muscles or bones (e.g., inflammation of the rib joints, arthritis of the spine), gastrointestinal tract (e.g., esophagitis, esophageal spasm, peptic ulcer, gall bladder disease, acute pancreatitis), lungs (e.g., lung emboli or clots, pneumonia, cancer), or may be due to heart or blood vessel problems other than coronary artery disease (e.g., inflammations of the heart or its enveloping sack, or narrowing of major blood vessels in the chest other than coronary arteries).

Why No Chest Pain in SMI?

Many people simply don't feel any pain when silent myocardial ischemia strikes. This may be the result of certain painkilling substances mysteriously produced by some people within their bodies, or it may be because of long-standing damage to nerve endings that occurs more frequently in diabetics or hypertensives, the two groups of patients who frequently suffer with SMI or have a high incidence of silent heart attacks.

Types of Silent Myocardial Ischemia

In April 1986, a group of prominent cardiologists met at the request of the National Heart Institute in Bethesda, Maryland. They defined silent myocardial ischemia and devised a classification system. Symptom-free patients without a history of heart disease, but who were afflicted with intermittently inadequate coronary artery blood flow, were henceforth to be called Type 1; patients with symptom-free SMI who had previously suffered a heart attack would be Type 2; and patients who were afflicted with anginal chest pains and SMI, but who had not previously suffered a heart attack, would be Type 3.

Type 1: Completely Silent

Jim Fixx—the famous marathon runner and author—died quite suddenly. Did he have angina? No. Did he have silent myocardial ischemia? Almost certainly, since it was subsequently demonstrated that he was afflicted with severe atherosclerotic narrowing of his three main coronary arteries, with an 85-percent narrowing of the right artery and significant narrowing of the arteries nourishing the left side of his heart. Also, he may previously have suffered a silent heart attack, and had very poor risk factors (male, age 52, previous cigarette smoker, high cholesterol, with a family history of heart disease). Yet he felt well enough to jog at the time of his death. He obviously had excellent secondary (i.e., collateral, or backup) coronary circulation (see Chapter 8), simply refused to acknowledge the presence of chest symptoms, and/or was endowed with an extremely high pain threshold. The presence of silent myocardial ischemia on treadmill testing or Holter recording would probably have shown up, even though enough blood coursed through his partially blocked coronary arteries to respond to any increased demand placed upon his heart by running. His death was quite likely caused by ventricular fibrillation, a malfunction of the heart's rhythm owing to sudden inadequacy of coronary artery blood flow. If SMI is diagnosed in a symptom-free patient, the outlook is as grave as it is for a similar patient whose SMI is accompanied by angina pains; in other words, SMI is bad whether or not it is associated with anginal chest pains.

Type 2: SMI in Patients After a Heart Attack

The million or so *annual* survivors of heart attacks in the United States form an extremely large, growing, and readily identifiable group of patients with *known* coronary heart disease. This group now totals at least 5 million. SMI is detected in these patients by exercise stress testing (see Chapter 10). Over the past decade it has become common practice to perform a *low level* stress test on a heart-attack subject one to three weeks after the attack has occurred. The cardiologist uses this test to ensure that patients are able to resume the increasingly vigorous physical activities required of them when they return home from the hospital without developing signs or symptoms suggestive of heart malfunctions. Routine and/or thallium stress testing (see Chapter 10) is also extensively employed weeks, months, and years after a heart attack in order to determine, first, the functional capacity of the heart (its ability to withstand an increased heart rate such as might occur in stressful or even relatively ordinary activities), and, second, whether or not silent myocardial ischemia is present.

Accurate statistics are very difficult to determine at present, but it has been estimated that at least 40 percent of the 1 million heart-attack survivors in the United States each year have abnormal tread-mill stress tests; some scientists have estimated that 50 percent of these will be totally without symptoms and that therefore, by defini-tion, these patients will be afflicted with silent myocardial ischemia. However, not all patients are able to be adequately tested on a treadmill after a heart attack for a variety of reasons: advanced age, obesity, orthopedic or pulmonary disease, presence of heart failure, or severe malfunctions of heart rhythm. Holter monitoring (see Chap-ter 10) in these patients reveals that as many as 33 percent have SMI. Post-heart-attack patients who demonstrate pain-free ischemia on either test have a much higher incidence of recurrent heart attacks, new onset of anginal chest pain, and sudden death than do patients who do not demonstrate SMI changes on these objective tests.

Patients afflicted with SMI after a heart attack are from three to ten times more likely to die within one year than are patients without SMI, and almost one-third of them do. Detecting SMI in these patients is important because it can be treated and the incidence of serious problems can thus be reduced or eliminated.

Type 3: SMI in Patients with Angina

The millions of Americans who have SMI *and* angina are more likely to have recurrent heart attacks, increasing angina, or even sudden death than are the angina patients without SMI. It is therefore of utmost importance to study, properly and carefully, *all* angina patients with treadmill testing and/or Holter recording in order to determine the presence of silent ischemia.

SMI occurs at least three to four times more frequently in angina patients than does ischemia with chest pain. Since the outlook for developing cardiac complications or sudden death is related to the presence and degree of ischemia, painful or not, the frequency of symptoms simply does not reflect the true severity of the coronary artery disease present in patients with chronic angina.

Patients with unstable angina are in a class by themselves; the probability of experiencing an acute heart attack or undergoing bypass heart surgery during the first 30 days after onset of unstable angina is significantly higher in patients who demonstrate SMI than it is in those who demonstrate little or no SMI.

The Significance of Chest Pain and SMI

SMI can be a lifesaving warning if detected. Symptom-free, high-risk SMI patients have a much higher mortality rate from heart attacks and sudden death than do patients without SMI. Patients with SMI who have previously suffered an acute heart attack and/or who have unstable angina are at *very high risk* for death and recurrent heart attacks as compared to similar patients without SMI.

It is vital that doctors identify which patients have symptom-free heart disease, because we now have specific therapies available that can delay or possibly even prevent heart attacks or sudden death. Although approximately 50 percent of all patients with significant heart disease go to their physicians because of chest pain or other symptoms, sudden death or an acute heart attack is *the* initial event for the other 50 percent. The vast majority of patients with symptom-free heart disease do not seek medical attention because they are totally unaware of their life-threatening heart condition.

Therefore, physicians and patients should *not* rely on chest pains as the first warning of a heart condition, since poor coronary artery blood flow occurs more frequently without than it does with chest pain. Since pain-free SMI is equally important as episodes associated with chest pain, or more so, physicians must direct their attention toward the early diagnosis and treatment of *all* episodes of coronary insufficiency, not just the painful ones.

3

The Silent Heart Attack

Coronary artery disease is a complex, multifaceted condition that often proceeds from a totally symptom-free state to an acute heart attack (or abrupt sudden death) with little or no warning. But heart attacks can also occur silently, without the patient's—or the doctor's—knowledge.

The standard resting electrocardiogram (EKG) is a simple test for demonstrating the presence of coronary heart disease; in fact, unequivocal evidence of a previous heart attack in totally symptom-free patients is an infrequent finding, but not a rare one, during the course of routine heart examinations, especially in certain groups of patients, such as hypertensives and diabetics. These unexpected heart attacks are considered to be "unrecognized" if they are detected by an EKG recorded during the course of a routine examination and if neither the patient nor his attending physicians has ever considered the possibility that a heart attack had occurred. Unrecognized heart attacks are classified as *truly silent* if the patient, even on careful questioning, does not recall experiencing any relevant chest pain or any other symptoms, even atypical ones.

When silent heart attacks are detected on screening examinations, about 50 percent are categorized as completely silent after the patient has been carefully questioned; the other 50 percent of patients remember atypical symptoms that may have signaled the heart attack—but they did not choose to seek medical attention, primarily because they did not feel that the symptoms were heart-related.

The Prevalence of Silent Heart Attacks

The incidence of silent heart attacks increases rapidly beyond the age of 45 in men and 55 in women. The occurrence of such attacks in women usually trails that in men by 20 years, but the gap closes with advancing age. Unrecognized heart attacks account for *at least* 25 to 30 percent (but may be as high as 60 percent) of *all* heart attacks.

Patients with unrecognized heart attacks tend to visit their physicians less often and commonly deny or negate symptoms that other patients would consider significant. The proportion of unrecognized heart attacks is higher in women (35 percent) than in men (28 percent); perhaps this means that women are more stoic or are biologically different in the way they experience and evaluate pain.

Why Is a Heart Attack Silent?

It is not completely clear why some heart attacks are painful and others are not. Current theory suggests that the reasons for the absence of pain in patients who suffer pain-free heart attacks are the same as for patients afflicted with silent myocardial ischemia (see Chapter 2). It is interesting to note that among patients who later develop angina pectoris, a greater number have had symptomatic, *recognized* heart attacks than have experienced *unrecognized* heart attacks. In other words, the latter group of patients, for whatever reasons, tend to perceive pain less frequently. Denial of symptoms and unwillingness to face the fact that a heart attack might be occurring almost certainly also contribute to the lack of symptom recognition.

Predisposing Factors for Silent Heart Attack

Diabetes and High Blood Pressure

If age and sex are not considered, there are few distinguishing characteristics in patients who are discovered to have suffered a silent heart attack. Except in the elderly, they are much more frequently found to have occurred in women than in men, and are more common in older men than in younger ones; the frequency does not vary greatly with age in women.

High blood pressure is the one major coronary risk factor that seems to be specifically related to unrecognized heart attacks, since as many as 50 percent of heart attacks in hypertensive women and 35 percent in hypertensive men are unrecognized. This result is rather startling, since hypertensive patients are usually more aware of the increased incidence of coronary heart problems in persons with their illness and tend to visit their physicians more frequently.

Completely silent or unrecognized heart attacks are much more common in diabetic than in nondiabetic patients. Also, diabetics complain of chest pain much less frequently than do nondiabetics during treadmill stress testing. One theory suggests that these differences may result from nerve fiber damage in the heart, produced by long-standing diabetes.

Survival

The outlook for patients who have suffered silent heart attacks is the same as it is for patients with a history of recognized, symptomatic heart attacks; if not treated, up to 50 percent of men and 34 percent of women will be dead within ten years. The rate of sudden heart deaths in these two groups of patients is also similar. These statistics can be improved significantly with medical treatment and careful attention to improvement or alteration of any abnormal risk factors (see Chapters 11 and 12).

Prevention

Because of the high incidence of unrecognized heart attacks, and because of their generally serious outlook, greater emphasis on prevention of coronary artery disease is needed to avoid this deceptively malignant condition. High-blood-pressure patients should especially be carefully monitored through routine examinations and electrocardiograms on a frequent and regular basis because of their increased incidence of silent heart attacks.

All other risk factors (see chapters 5, 11, and 12) should be identified and vigorously treated; for example, cessation of cigarette smoking has been shown to reduce the incidence of recurrent fatal heart attacks, sudden death, and overall death rates by 20 to 50 percent. Women over the age of 35 should discontinue the use of oral contraceptives, especially if they smoke cigarettes or have other abnormal risk factors. Careful medical follow-up examinations and appropriate treatments are necessary for the remainder of the silent-heart-attack victim's life, just as it would be for someone who had suffered a routine, painful heart attack, to reduce the incidence of recurrent heart injuries or sudden death.

C H A P T E R

4

Sudden Death:
The Silent Killer Stalks

Totally unexpected death occurring within one hour of the onset of symptoms in a victim with or without known, preexisting heart disease is called sudden cardiac death (SCD). It is responsible for up to 20 percent of all natural fatalities in the industrially developed world.

The usual cause of sudden death is an abnormal heart rhythm called *ventricular fibrillation*, which, if not promptly treated, causes death within three to four minutes. This chaotic rhythm, the most serious of all *arrhythmias*, consists of a completely disorganized quivering pattern of pumping activity, resulting from attempts by many parts of the heart to contract simultaneously; the heart looks and acts like a beached jellyfish. Coordinated contraction is impossible, and as a result, pumping of blood from the heart into the circulatory system ceases. In a coronary care unit, in an emergency room, or even when a trained paramedic in the field finds this abnormal rhythm to be present, the heart frequently can be restored to normal rhythm using a defibrillator, a device that sends a controlled electric shock to the heart.

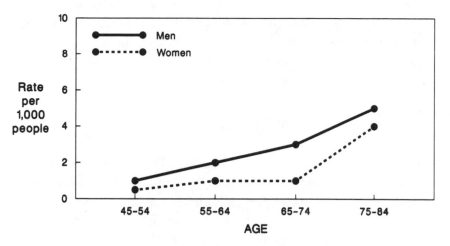

Figure 7. **Incidence of sudden death in persons free of coronary heart disease.** *Source: Framingham Heart Study, 30-year follow-up.*

Incidence and Cause

Sudden deaths increase in frequency with increasing age, even though symptoms suggestive of heart trouble may never have been present (see Figure 7). The peak incidence occurs between ages 75 and 84. It is four times more common in men than in women, possibly because men do not have the same protection from coronary artery disease enjoyed by premenopausal women.

Although there are hundreds of causes of sudden death, coronary atherosclerosis is by far the most frequent underlying abnormality found to be present in sudden death victims. Approximately one-half of the people who die suddenly have previously suffered heart attacks (frequently silent), and only 20 to 27 percent of the episodes are caused by a new heart attack.

A U.S. Public Health Service study conducted among the residents of the town of Framingham, Massachusetts, since 1948 reported that sudden death was the first symptom or event in about 20 percent of all coronary heart disease patients. Think of what that means—one out of every five people who develop a heart problem will die suddenly. Death is the first and last sign of their heart disease: they never knew what hit them; they never even suspected that they had a heart problem. During the first 30 years of the Framingham study, half of the men and almost two-thirds of the women who died suddenly had no previous history of coronary heart disease.

Who's at Risk?

Patients at higher risk of sudden death include those with known coronary artery disease or cardiomyopathy (an illness complicated by significantly abnormal heart function and heart failure), and patients who are obese, have high blood pressure or high cholesterol, smoke cigarettes, or have frequent or complex abnormalities of heart rhythm. The risk increases significantly when more risk factors are present (see Figure 8 in Chapter 5). Once heart disease is found to be present, the risk of sudden death increases ninefold.

Causes of Sudden Death

Since an acute or new heart attack is responsible for sudden death in only about one-fourth of the victims, the majority of episodes appear to be caused by the same transient risk factors (see Chapter 2) responsible for SMI. When these factors come into play, they increase the likelihood of coronary artery blockage that may result in increased irritability of the heart, arrhythmia (ventricular fibrillation), and . . . sudden death. However, rhythm abnormalities and sudden death may also be caused by factors other than poor coronary artery blood flow. It has been postulated, for example, that biochemical or hormonal abnormalities might increase sympathetic nervous system activity in the morning hours, causing electrical instability of the heart that could result in ventricular fibrillation and sudden death. These transient risk factors (which should be distinguished from the well-known common risk factors discussed in Chapter 5) are especially important to identify, since it is possible to effectively treat them, thereby reducing the incidence of sudden deaths or heart attacks.

The Circadian Rhythm of Sudden Cardiac Death

As does SMI, nonfatal heart attacks are much more likely to occur in the morning than at other times of the day. At least 13 out of 14 scientific studies have clearly demonstrated that the peak onset of heart attacks and sudden death occurs between 6:00 A.M. and noon. The Massachusetts Department of Public Health and the Framingham Heart Study reported similar data, and in addition, the latter group noted that the risk of sudden cardiac death was at least 70 percent greater between 7:00 and 9:00 A.M. than during the remaining 22 hours of the day.

Sudden Death in Youth

Philosophically, some people consider death to be premature, no matter at what age it occurs. However, contrasted with the sudden death of someone who is middle-aged or older, sudden death of a young person is universally considered premature, tragic, and emotionally devastating, since it is never expected. The frequency of these episodes in youthful athletes in the United States is *extremely* rare, especially considering that millions of these competitors are involved in athletic activities each day in the United States.

Although accidents, suicide, and drugs are the most frequent overall causes of death in persons under the age of 30, abnormalities of the heart or its blood vessels are the usual cause of youthful sudden death. Persons over the age of 30 who die suddenly, whether athletic or sedentary, usually have previously been totally symptom-free and, in the vast majority of instances, are found to have premature aging of the coronary arteries owing to atherosclerosis, with resultant narrowing or complete blockage of these important vessels.

Symptoms to Look For, and Events Preceding Sudden Death

Patients who die suddenly, whether or not risk factors have been identified and/or treated, may have significant symptoms that precede the event and that should alert both the patient and his or her doctor to the increased risk of sudden death. Unfortunately, many of these early symptoms are vague and nonspecific.

Even though as many as 33 percent of heart attack victims had consulted their physicians because of new or increasing chest pains in the six months before the heart injury occurred, chest pain is a relatively infrequent symptom, occurring in no more than 10 percent of cases of sudden death. Shortness of breath, weakness or fatigue, chest palpitations, and a variety of other relatively imprecise complaints, such as indigestion, back pains, or pains in the shoulders, arms, or hands, and so on, occur more frequently; even though vague, these symptoms frequently are of sufficient intensity to bring the patient to his physician days or weeks before the final event. As many as 46 percent of sudden heart death victims had preexisting complaints severe enough to have caused them to see a physician within four weeks prior to death. In fact, many of these patients had visited their doctors only three to four hours prior to the event.

What to Do

Because significant *treatable* abnormalities of heart rhythm were detected prior to the occurrence of sudden death in approximately 85 percent of the out-of-hospital survivors, you should consult your physician as soon as possible after the onset of any significant symptoms. The greatest danger to a patient with an acute heart attack or premonitory symptoms of sudden death is *denial*. Negation of personal danger by denial, one of the most common human reactions to situations of life stress, is similar to rationalization; that is, it is a patient's unconscious attempt to minimize or eliminate the threat to his life or health. Denial leads to delay (the time elapsed from the onset of symptoms to the arrival at a medical facility), and *the average delay time ranges from 2.9 to 5.1 hours*. The gravity of this problem becomes apparent when one realizes that at least 50 percent of all deaths from heart attacks occur within four hours of the onset of symptoms, usually before the patient reaches the hospital. Even among survivors of an acute heart attack, the size of the heart attack, and therefore the severity of subsequent complications, appears to be related to delay in treatment; patients simply do not get to well-equipped medical facilities in time to prevent major problems.

Those who recognize the true causes of their symptoms will get to the hospital sooner than those who explain away their symptoms as being due to a "stomachache" or "muscle spasm." Husbands and wives are responsible for producing more delay than are friends, associates, and employers. *Denial and delay must be avoided if the incidence of sudden death is to be reduced.*

Specific drug treatments and other therapies that can reduce or often completely eliminate the potential of sudden death are available to patients who present themselves quickly enough to a hospital emergency room. Chest pain of new onset, any change in a long-standing pattern (i.e., either the frequency or the intensity) of chest discomfort, or even atypical chest symptoms known as *anginal equivalents* (pains occurring in the teeth, jaw, neck, shoulders, or back, or in the arms, elbows, or fingers) should cause one to seek immediate medical attention. Also, even vague symptoms such as shortness of breath, weakness or fatigue, or recurrent palpitations should not be ignored, especially if precipitated by minimal exertion.

Physicians should be consulted as frequently as is necessary to evaluate symptoms and answer questions, especially by persons who are at high risk. Prevention and treatment of abnormal risk factors will effectively reduce the incidence of sudden death. So let's see what risk is all about.

5

Are You Living on Borrowed Time?

You and your doctor can launch a preemptive attack on the invisible enemy, silent heart disease, before it makes its appearance as a heart attack or sudden cardiac death.

We start by carefully screening symptom-free patients for coronary heart disease, but we can't screen everyone. It is scientific nonsense to subject a healthy, 22-year-old man to extensive cardiac screening procedures (unless he is an athlete or will be exercising vigorously), because the likelihood of detecting significant coronary artery disease is extremely low. On the other hand, since coronary artery disease increases in frequency with increasing age, it is entirely appropriate to screen, for example, a symptom-free man for this problem, even if he is only 40 years old, especially if he possesses one or more of the important risk factors known to be associated with the premature development of coronary artery disease (see Figure 8).

People who develop coronary heart problems frequently tend to have similar features in their family history, health picture, and lifestyle. Such features are known as *risk factors*. Extensive clinical and statistical studies have clearly identified the factors associated with an increased susceptibility to heart attack and stroke, but it should be recognized that not everyone who has these risk factors will actually develop these diseases. Some factors have proven to be significant all by themselves, whereas others are individually less

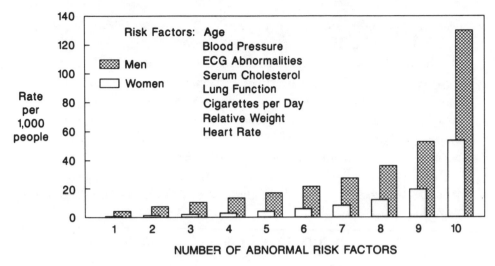

Figure 8.   Risk of sudden death by number of abnormal risk factors present. *Source: Framingham Heart Study, 26-year follow-up.*

important but become more meaningful when associated with other specific risk factors in the same person (see Figure 8). An understanding of the importance of these coronary risk factors and their potentially fatal combinations, or *synergies*, is the key to the early detection of coronary heart disease. If abnormal risk factors can be altered or improved, atherosclerotic plaque formation may be prevented, its growth retarded, or its size actually reduced. The net result will be to retard, delay, or prevent symptomatic coronary heart disease, heart attacks, and/or sudden death.

Which Risk Factors Are Important?

The four most significant coronary risk factors are heredity or family history, cigarette smoking, high blood pressure, and elevated blood cholesterol. Other, less significant, risk factors are being male, growing older, having diabetes, being obese or under unusual stress, and lacking in exercise; recently, several of these so-called less important risk factors have been demonstrated to be more important than was originally thought, and in fact they appear to have a similar degree of significance as smoking, high blood pressure and elevated cholesterol. The more risk factors that are present, the greater the chance that a person will develop heart disease (see Figure 9). Therefore we should make every effort to improve or eliminate abnormal risk factors that can be changed to delay or prevent the onset of symptomatic heart disease, even if it is supposedly predestined to occur because of an abnormal genetic pattern.

Risk factors are basically of two varieties: those over which we have absolutely no control, and those that we can minimize or eliminate.

Risk Factors That Cannot Be Changed

Family History

Unless significant changes are made in his or her health and living patterns, a person has a genetically predestined tendency for developing coronary artery disease if a close relative (i.e., father, mother, sibling) had developed symptomatic coronary artery disease prior to the age of 55 or, according to some authorities, 60. Highly regarded scientific studies have demonstrated that while strong genetic forces may predispose a person to develop symptomatic heart disease, important environmental factors help actually initiate the process and precipitate the end result. What's important is that in many cases, identification and modification of these harmful environmental factors may prevent or delay an early heart attack or even sudden death. For example, a person's specific genetic makeup can elevate his cholesterol level abnormally, two to three times above normal. This occurs in a condition known as *familial hypercholesterolemia*, which affects only 0.5 percent of the general population. The cholesterol level in a 40-year-old patient with this problem could range between 350 and 450 mg/dl, and if the person is a male, the chances for an early heart attack are virtually 100 percent unless something is done about it. It should be noted that the pioneer ancestors of these unfortunate individuals, persons living three to five

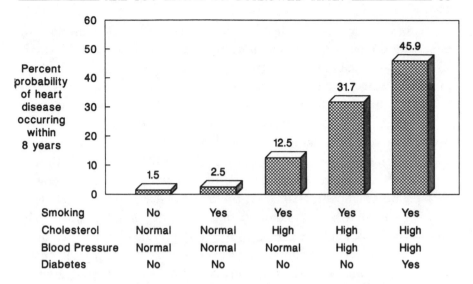

Figure 9. Effect of added risk factors on incidence of disease in a
40-year-old man. *Source: Framingham Heart Study.*

generations back, in the mid-1800s, at a time when eating habits, exercise patterns, and lifestyles were much better than they are today, frequently survived into their sixties and seventies. In fact, some of these ancestors even survived into their eighties with the same genetic pattern that currently kills their great-grandsons in their thirties and forties, because the latter have made the mistake of permitting their blood cholesterol levels to remain high.

An abnormal genetic pattern places a person in the ballpark of risk; a variety of environmental factors will move them around within that ballpark. For example, persons with genetically high levels of cholesterol (over 300–400 mg/dl) will almost certainly have an early coronary event unless their cholesterol is lowered with diet or medication or both. Minimal or moderate elevations of blood cholesterol levels do not cause a coronary event by themselves, but become important if other factors, such as cigarette smoking, high blood pressure, or diabetes are present. A fortunate 10 percent of the population have cholesterol levels that are so low that even if they smoke cigarettes or are hypertensive, they probably won't develop a coronary problem.

Factors other than cholesterol levels may also have important effects on the early development of heart disease in those individuals afflicted with the genetic abnormality noted above. There are families in which as many as seven relatives suffered early heart attacks, and in fact, in one reported family, two of the seven heart attack victims were women only 30 and 40 years old. Besides their abnormal family history, the only common risk factor they shared was that they were all cigarette smokers. It seems quite probable that these unfortunate individuals inherited a basic genetic defect, which, when associated with cigarette smoking, triggered the onset of early coronary disease. Some geneticists have concluded that cigarette smoking is the *primary* risk factor that triggers a preexisting genetic abnormality in as many as 30 percent of families whose members develop early heart attacks. High blood pressure is considered to be a genetic trigger in 25 percent of early-heart-attack families, and abnormal serum fat patterns (elevated serum cholesterol levels, etc.) are noted to be present and are thought to be the genetic trigger in another 25 percent of families. Therefore, approximately 80 percent of individuals who have a family history of premature heart disease and who develop early coronary insufficiency are afflicted with specific risk factors *that can be treated*. If these people are treated in time, premature coronary heart disease and sudden death can be avoided.

A family history of heart disease is present in as many as 66 percent of patients who have a proven heart attack or who develop other forms of heart disease before the age of 55. Because of the extremely strong influence of the family history in these individuals, it is of major importance to screen, through complete history and physical examination, blood tests, and treadmill stress test, all close relatives of premature heart attack or sudden-death victims carefully in an attempt to uncover and then to initiate treatment of early, silent heart disease.

Before we leave the subject of family history, it is necessary to emphasize a particularly important point. If a young man comes to a hospital emergency room with vague chest pain, it's not highly likely that he's suffering a heart attack. But if that same young man has close relatives who have histories of early heart attacks, especially if he is a cigarette smoker, even if an acute heart attack is ruled out by the routine tests performed in the emergency room, it is definitely worthwhile to consider further diagnostic testing. He should have a treadmill stress test because his family history is a much more predictive risk factor than are the negative or inconclusive findings of a normal resting electrocardiogram and physical examination.

Male Sex

Men are at significantly greater risk of developing heart disease than are women, especially women under the age of 50. The incidence of heart attacks increases in women after menopause, as they lose the protective effects of the female hormones produced by their ovaries during their reproductive years. Men are ten times more likely to develop a heart attack than are females prior to the age of 45, seven times more likely in the 55-to-64-year-old group, but only twice as likely in the 65-to-74-year-old age group; women start to catch up as they get older. Despite the striking increase in heart problems after menopause, the death rate in women is still not as great as in men; consequently, in the Western world, women have a life span averaging eight years longer than men.

Because of these sex-linked differences (which suggest that premenopausal women are protected from coronary heart problems because of their high female hormone levels), a number of scientific studies have been mounted to determine whether female hormones (estrogens) administered to both men and women would reduce the incidence of heart attacks. Results indicate that estrogen use in postmenopausal women may protect against the development of coronary artery disease. But this protective effect is lost if abnormal risk factors, such as cigarette smoking, elevated cholesterol, and obesity, are present. When estrogens were given to men, they did not appear to be protective; in fact, they seemed to increase the frequency of cardiovascular problems.

Increasing Age

The incidence of heart attacks is definitely age-related, increasing in frequency in the older age groups. Approximately 55 percent of all heart-attack victims are 65 years of age or older, and of those who die as a result of heart attacks, almost 80 percent are over the age of 65.

Major Risk Factors That Can Be Changed

Cigarette Smoking

Cigarette smoking is the worst health hazard in America today, and has a greater impact on health than does any other known risk factor. The Surgeon General of the United States has proclaimed that cigarette smoking is the most important preventable risk factor for cardiovascular disease. Patients who smoke, especially those who have elevated blood pressure and/or serum cholesterol levels, may have up to ten times greater chance of developing a heart attack than do those patients who do not have these risk factors. The Surgeon General emphasizes that approximately 250,000 lives are being lost annually in the United States because of the cardiac effects of cigarette smoking, and that many of these could be saved if smoking were eliminated (see Figure 10). He has also declared cigarette smoking to be responsible for approximately 80,000 deaths annually from lung cancer, and the habit has been associated with other diseases such as emphysema, chronic bronchitis, bladder cancer, strokes, and circulatory problems in the legs.

After the Surgeon General's first report in 1964 linking lung cancer and heart disease to cigarette smoking, the number of smokers in the adult population dropped, but some 50 million Americans still smoke cigarettes on a regular basis. Whereas 52 percent of American men smoked in 1964, this percentage is now down to 35 percent. There has been a similar but less dramatic drop in women, from 35 percent to 30 percent. Yet, for a variety of psychological and social reasons,

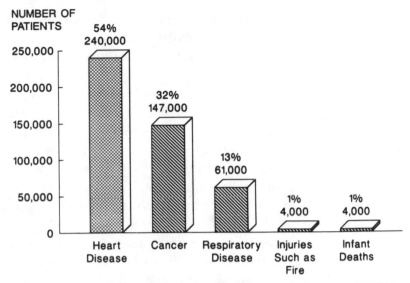

CAUSES OF DEATH DUE TO CIGARETTE SMOKING, PER YEAR

Figure 10. Cigarette smoking causes more deaths due to heart disease than all other categories combined.

women in the 17-to-35 age group appear to be smoking more rather than less.

The Killer Addiction

Although the damaging effects of cigarette smoking had been known for many years, it was not until after the 1964 Surgeon General's report that all cigarette packages were required to carry the famous warning label that read, WARNING: THE SURGEON GENERAL HAS DETERMINED THAT CIGARETTE SMOKING MAY BE HAZARDOUS TO YOUR HEALTH. This report concluded that tobacco was a serious health hazard, but defined smoking as a "habit," not an addiction. Each annual report since then has clearly reinforced the conclusion that smoking is a major public health hazard, a "habit" with disastrous consequences. The latest report, released in May 1988 by Surgeon General C. Everett Koop, is a one-and-a-half-inch-thick treatise titled *Health Consequences of Smoking: Nicotine Addiction*. He drew upon the advice of more than 2,000 scientific papers and more than 50 medical experts to conclude that nicotine had mood-altering effects, that it promoted consistent and repetitive patterns of use, and that continued use would lead to "tolerance," with the need to increase the dose.

This report received unanimous accolades from the political as well as the medical community since, *for the first time*, the Surgeon General had clearly concluded that cigarettes and other forms of tobacco were addictive and further urged that they be treated with the same caution as illegal street narcotics. He indicated that 75 to 85 percent of the nation's 51 million smokers would like to quit, but had been unable to do so. He reported that cessation led to withdrawal symptoms including irritability, poor concentration, and sleep disorders, that the effect of nicotine in cigarette smoke was similar to the effects of other drugs, and that it was "driven by strong, often irresistible urges and [could] persist despite repeated efforts to quit."

The conclusion of the report was that nicotine, the most active ingredient in tobacco, was every bit as addicting as heroin and cocaine. He recommended strong public-health actions, including placement of warning labels regarding addiction on packages of tobacco products, a ban on cigarette vending machines in order to curb availability to children, and tighter regulation of tobacco sales through licensing.

Effects of Smoking on Health and Life

Cigarette smoking is one of the three major risk factors for heart attacks and strokes. If a cigarette smoker has both high blood pressure and high blood cholesterol, his risk of developing symptomatic coronary heart problems is ten times that of a nonsmoker without high blood pressure or elevated serum cholesterol.

Cigarette smoking is particularly bad for the lungs, as it causes a progressive deterioration of all respiratory functions. It is the leading cause of emphysema, chronic lung disease, and chronic bronchitis; it increases the risk of lung cancer by a factor of 20, and also is a major factor in cancers of the upper respiratory tree (the mouth, larynx, and throat). It also has been implicated in cancers at other locations, including the esophagus, stomach, kidneys, pancreas, and bladder, and is an addiction shared by many hypertensive patients.

Scientists have now been able to calculate exactly what each cigarette costs in terms of life. The death rate increase depends on the number of cigarettes smoked daily, and the length of time that the person has been smoking. The harmful effect of cigarettes is puff-related; that is, each puff increases the damage. In effect, even though smoking less than ten cigarettes per day is better than smoking 20 per day, there is no safe level of smoking, nor is there such a thing as a safe cigarette. Smoking one package a day for 15 years will result in a loss of 20 seconds of life per cigarette. It adds up quickly: a two-pack-a-day smoker will die approximately eight years earlier than he should, or even sooner if he develops premature coronary artery disease. Persons who smoke a pack of cigarettes a day have more than twice the risk of heart attacks of people who have never smoked; smoking 40 cigarettes a day or more increases the risk of heart attack by at least three times. Cigarette smoking causes almost 500,000 deaths each year (see Figure 10), a number that is over 12 times the annual deaths from auto accidents, and would be the equivalent of four fully loaded 747 jet airliners crashing each day. Pipe and cigar smokers, who do not inhale, have only a minimal increase in heart-related deaths, compared to nonsmokers.

Do Filters Work?

Most scientists do not believe that cigarettes reputed to produce less nicotine and tar because of "more effective" filters are safer than regular cigarettes. The Framingham study demonstrated that filter cigarette smokers may even have a higher incidence of coronary heart disease than smokers of nonfiltered cigarettes; the study implied that smokers who switch to lower-nicotine cigarettes very likely inhale more deeply, take larger puffs, and perhaps smoke the cigarettes longer in order to compensate for the presumably lower level of nicotine. Cigarette filtration therefore does not reduce or eliminate the damaging cardiac effects of this noxious and toxic habit.

What's in Smoke

Although tobacco smoke contains more than 4,000 components, the most dangerous constituents are nicotine and carbon monoxide. Moreover, it has been reported that a 20-cigarette-per-day smoker will inhale *one cup of pure tar* into his or her lungs during the course of one year.

The carbon monoxide in cigarette smoke deprives the tissues, including the heart muscle, of oxygen; in addition, it almost certainly contributes to the formation of blood clotting within the coronary arteries, which eventually leads to angina and heart attacks. Filters do not prevent carbon monoxide from reaching the lungs.

Nicotine

Nicotine is a powerful, *addictive* drug, which, when inhaled, rapidly passes through the air-filled sacs of the lung tissue and enters the bloodstream. It takes only seven to ten seconds to reach the brain (three times faster than an ingested drug and at least as fast as an intravenous drug), and it frequently makes the smoker more alert, able to think faster. Besides stimulating the adrenal glands to put out adrenaline, nicotine itself mimics many of the actions of adrenaline and another drug, *acetylcholine*, a powerful drug that influences the brain. Cigarette smokers soon become dependent; their addiction requires them to keep a continuous supply of nicotine circulating in the bloodstream. If they attempt to stop smoking permanently or even for a short time, they may experience unpleasant symptoms of cigarette withdrawal, including irritability, unusual cravings, inability to concentrate, insomnia, fatigue, sleepiness, headache, nausea, and anxiety—in other words, all of the symptoms that we frequently see in the personality makeup of cigarette smokers (or drug addicts). In some people, nicotine tends to produce a calming effect by releasing natural opiate-like products called *beta-endorphins*. Because of these mixed signals, the biological system may become confused; a smoker can therefore demonstrate either or both of two states of mind, of alertness (frequently manifested as irritability) on the one hand and relaxation on the other.

Nicotine cannot be stored in the body; the supply in the blood-stream must be constantly renewed, which is why cigarette smoking is addictive. By taking 200 to 400 puffs a day, a relatively constant level of nicotine is maintained in the bloodstream, and as a result, there is a great deal of pharmacological as well as psychological reinforcement. Nicotine is powerfully addicting because it is a self-administered substance that controls mood and performance, and, unfortunately, it is a legal drug.

Short-Term Effects of Nicotine

In addition to its addictive and behavioral effects, nicotine exerts acute effects on the cardiovascular system. The nicotine in even a few puffs of a cigarette will rapidly increase the heart rate and blood pressure, effectively increasing the heart's workload. It narrows blood vessels all over the body, frequently diminishing the arterial circulation to the arms and legs, leading to severe circulatory disorders often requiring surgical correction, usually in the legs. It suppresses the appetite for sugar, relaxes the muscles of the body, and frequently causes a sensation of chilliness. It increases the excitability of the heart, which may cause *extrasystoles* (premature beats) or more serious malfunctions of heart rhythm. Sudden cardiac death resulting from a heart arrhythmia is much more common in heavy cigarette smokers than in the nonsmoking population. One recent scientific study found that SMI was six times more frequent and lasted seven times longer in smokers than in nonsmokers.

Long-Term Effects of Cigarette Smoking

The major deleterious effects of cigarette smoking usually occur many years after the first cigarette is lit. There are a variety of explanations for its long-term actions. Some scientists have demonstrated significant damage to the internal lining of the coronary arteries, possibly caused by an excess of carbon monoxide in the blood. Cigarette smoking increases blood viscosity or thickness and tends to make certain blood elements (platelets) more sticky and adherent, making the blood flow more sluggish and thereby increasing its tendency to form a coronary thrombosis or clot.

The fat metabolism of the body is disturbed by cigarette smoking. Among the major components it affects are *high-density lipoproteins* (HDL), a component of cholesterol that, in the view of many scientists, acts to protect against the development of atherosclerosis, and therefore, the higher the level of HDL, the better. The Framingham study revealed a lower level of HDL among smokers, related primarily to the number of cigarettes smoked per day. (Interestingly, the HDL level also tended to be lower in cigar or pipe smokers who formerly had been cigarette smokers, apparently because these smokers were different from most cigar and pipe smokers; that is, they had a greater tendency to inhale the smoke, regardless of its source.) Cigarette smokers who discontinue the habit for at least one year return to the same HDL level as nonsmokers. For some unknown reason, women smokers tend to have lower HDL levels than do male smokers, which may be the reason why 75 percent of the heart attacks suffered by otherwise healthy women under the age of 50 occur in cigarette smokers.

Health Hazard to Others

Cigarette smoking poses a serious health problem to persons other than smokers themselves. A burning cigarette produces *mainstream smoke*, which is inhaled into the lungs of the smoker and then exhaled; the smoke that comes off the burning end of the cigarette or is exhaled by the smoker is called *side-stream* smoke. When a non-smoker breathes air contaminated by side-stream smoke, it is called passive smoking; such air contains a wide variety of the same materials which are inhaled in mainstream smoke. Although the effects of passive smoking are most devastating to children, it has been increasingly recognized that nonsmoking adults working, living, or traveling in a smoke-filled environment are at risk for developing all of the complications and problems that affect cigarette smokers at an earlier age than do nonsmokers who have not been exposed to passive smoke; in fact, major public-health measures have recently been enacted in states and cities across the United States to protect the nonsmoker from passive inhalation.

Will Stopping Smoking Help?

But why should one stop smoking? Hasn't the damage already been done? No. It has been clearly demonstrated that a smoker's risk of experiencing a future heart attack starts to decrease toward the risk level of a nonsmoker within six months after smoking has been stopped, reaches 50 percent of the risk of nonsmokers within one to two years, and approaches risk levels equal to those of nonsmokers within five to ten years. No matter what it takes to quit, the short-term and long-term benefits far outweigh the limited period of anguish that accompanies kicking the habit.

High Blood Pressure

Blood pressure is a measure of the force that circulates the blood through the body. It has two components: the first and higher number, the *systolic* blood pressure, is the pressure in the arteries when the left ventricle ejects the blood into the aorta. The lower number, the *diastolic* pressure, is the pressure in the arteries when the left ventricle is relaxing between beats, filling up with more blood.

High blood pressure, or *hypertension,* is considered to be present when the systolic reading is higher than 140 mm of mercury and the diastolic greater than 90 mm. Initial readings obtained by a doctor or nurse are often relatively high, usually because of a patient's anxiety associated with a visit to a doctor; it is therefore important to obtain repeated readings before concluding that blood pressure is abnormal.

Blood pressure varies significantly from person to person; in fact, even in the same person, it may vary depending upon body position (lying, sitting, or standing), degree of emotional stress, and level of physical activity. When one is sleeping or resting, blood pressure tends to be lower than when one is exercising.

Incidence

Over 59 million Americans have high blood pressure. Black Americans have a 33-percent greater chance of having hypertension than do whites. Heart attacks are five times more frequent in patients with abnormally high blood pressure. Most individuals with high blood pressure do not have symptoms, and therefore it is frequently not detected before complications affecting the heart, kidney, brain, or blood vessels develop; for this reason, it is often referred to as "the silent killer."

What Are the Dangers?

High blood pressure predisposes one to the earlier development of atherosclerosis involving a number of critical organs; as a result, premature coronary artery disease leading to early (and often silent) heart attacks is more common in hypertensive patients. Elevated blood pressure causes the heart to work much harder than normal to pump blood against the higher resistance; over many years, this increased burden may cause enlargement of the heart, and eventually the heart will fail to function efficiently as a pump, resulting in a condition known as congestive heart failure. When congestive heart failure develops, the heart is unable to pump an adequate amount of blood to the body, and complications affecting the lungs, kidneys, and other organs may occur. High blood pressure is also a major factor in the development of strokes, kidney failure, and visual disturbances. In fact, it may affect the circulation to virtually every major organ in the body.

Detection and Treatment

The detection of hypertension is simplicity itself—all that is needed is to have one's blood pressure taken. Treatment depends upon the cause of the blood pressure elevation, but in over 90 percent of cases, the exact cause cannot be determined; these patients are classified as having *"essential" hypertension*. Regardless of the exact cause of elevated blood pressure in any individual, it is important to recognize that it is easy to detect and, most important, equally easy to treat. In the early 1960s, only one out of ten hypertensive patients in this country was adequately treated, but by the early 1980s, three out of four were well controlled.

Patients with high blood pressure should help themselves by reducing the amount of salt in their diets, losing weight, avoiding excess alcohol intake, and eliminating or modifying emotional stress.

The many medications available to lower blood pressure will be thoroughly reviewed in Chapter 12. These include *diuretics*, which reduce salt (sodium) and excess body fluid; *beta-blockers*, which reduce heart rate and the output of blood from the heart; *sympathetic nerve inhibitors*, which limit the ability of these nerves to narrow blood vessels (and therefore the vessels dilate or open up); *vasodilators*, which actively dilate the blood vessels in the fingers and toes, thereby decreasing blood pressure; and, finally, a relatively new class of drugs known as *ACE inhibitors*, which lower blood pressure by interfering with the body's production of *angiotensin*, a chemical that causes the arteries to constrict, resulting in a rise in blood pressure.

High Blood Cholesterol

Cholesterol is a fatty, yellowish substance that has been demonstrated to be a major component of arteriosclerotic plaques. It is present in many of the foods that we eat (e.g., dairy products, shellfish, egg yolks, meat), and is also normally manufactured by the liver. It is carried in the bloodstream in the form of large protein molecules called *lipoproteins*.

Very-low-density lipoproteins (VLDL) transport cholesterol as well as other fatty substances called triglycerides in the bloodstream. When the triglycerides are used up, the VLDL becomes the cholesterol-rich (and triglyceride-poor) substance called *low-density lipoprotein* (LDL). Most of the cholesterol in the bloodstream resides in these LDL particles, and therefore a high level of LDL will usually be present when the cholesterol level is high; elevated levels of these substances will increase fatty-acid buildup in the arteries and will contribute to premature development of atheriosclerotic lesions on the arterial walls.

Cholesterol is also carried in another lipoprotein known as *high-density lipoprotein* (HDL). The function of this lipoprotein is to remove cholesterol from body cells and deliver it to the liver, where it can be metabolized and eventually eliminated. Since the HDL particle removes cholesterol, it actually protects the arteries against atheriosclerosis; it is therefore better to have a high level of these particles in the bloodstream. High HDL and low cholesterol levels will result in a favorably *low* HDL/cholesterol ratio.

Many other complex events occur in cholesterol-LDL-triglyceride-VLDL metabolism, but cholesterol and LDL should be clearly identified as the villains and HDL as the hero.

There are two major types of cholesterol problems: in the first type, some individuals lack the means to get the cholesterol and its carrier (LDL) out of the blood properly; in the second, too much cholesterol and lipoproteins are produced. In either case, too much unused cholesterol is left behind in the bloodstream, and the excess tends to accumulate on the arterial walls, eventually clogging the arteries to a dangerous extent, or even a lethal one.

Cholesterol Levels in Other Countries

Historically, the rate of coronary artery disease was always much lower in Japan (although the rate has risen dramatically over the past

40 years) and the Mediterranean countries than in the United States and the Netherlands; this probably occurred because the percentage of calories consumed from unhealthy saturated fats and cholesterol was significantly lower in Japan and in the Mediterranean countries. In these studies, the average cholesterol level in Japan was 170 mg/dl, whereas in Finland it was in the range of 275 mg/dl. The excessive consumption of dairy products presumably caused the elevated levels in the Finns, resulting in a coronary death rate six times higher in Finland than in Japan. When the cholesterol in the Finnish diet was reduced, the incidence of heart attacks dropped by 42 percent.

Cholesterol Level and Heart Disease

A significant correlation exists between the level of serum cholesterol and the risk of developing coronary heart disease. The Framingham study clearly identified elevated serum cholesterol levels as one of the primary risk factors for the development of coronary atherosclerosis. Similar results were noted in the Coronary Primary Prevention Trial (CPPT) carried out in twelve clinics across North America, which screened over 300,000 men; medication was effective in reducing serum cholesterol by 9 percent, with a resulting decrease in coronary heart disease of 19 percent.

In 1987 a panel of national experts in blood cholesterol control was convened by the National Heart, Lung and Blood Institute in Bethesda, Maryland. Its purpose was to update and add more specific recommendations to basic policies set forth by previous expert committees such as the 1984 National Institutes of Health Consensus Panel. The panel had concluded that the available evidence "established beyond a reasonable doubt that lowering definitely elevated blood cholesterol (specifically, blood levels of the low-density lipoprotein, LDL) will reduce the risk of heart attacks caused by coronary artery disease" and "that the high blood levels of most Americans are undesirably high, in large part because of a high dietary intake of calories, saturated fat, and cholesterol."

The 1987 NIH panel reviewed the 1984 recommendations for detection and treatment of elevated cholesterol levels. It proposed that all adults, regardless of age, with blood cholesterol levels of 240 mg/dl or higher should receive medical evaluation, treatment, and follow-up; that those with blood cholesterol levels of 200 to 239 mg/dl should receive similar treatment if other risk characteristics were present; and that those with levels lower than 200 mg/dl were to be considered in a "desirable" range. Treatment decisions were also recommended based on the blood levels of LDL cholesterol: levels of less than 130 mg/dl were considered desirable; levels of 130 to 159 mg/dl were defined as "borderline high risk"; and levels of 160 mg/dl and higher were classified as "high risk." If other risk factors were present, an LDL level of only 130 mg/dl or greater also fell into the high risk category.

Two basic approaches for reducing the risk of cholesterol in the population were recommended. One was aimed at identifying persons with high blood cholesterol or low-density lipoprotein levels, treating them with diet and, if necessary, drugs. The second approach was a mass-strategy one, aimed at changing the dietary habits of the population as a whole, in an attempt to achieve a universal lowering of serum cholesterol levels; a national effort is now being mounted to educate adults and children into making informed dietary choices with this view in mind. Finally, it was recommended that children of high-risk families, such as those with histories of early heart attack, hypertension, diabetes, or abnormally elevated serum fats, should be screened at an early age for elevated cholesterol.

One final comment is necessary at this point since the overall relationship of cholesterol to coronary artery disease is not clearly understood even at this late date. In fact, as indicated earlier, one component of the total serum cholesterol, the high-density lipoproteins (HDL), even appears to play a vital role in preventing rather than causing coronary heart disease; the members of some 50 families in and around Cincinnati, Ohio, live long lives apparently protected by their high HDL values, regardless of what they eat. In other words, the final statement regarding the relationship of cholesterol to heart disease cannot be made as yet; we should all keep an open mind. But, except in the case of HDL, no one has ever said that cholesterol is good for you and therefore, for the time being, every attempt should be made to get the total cholesterol and LDL levels as low as possible, certainly below 200 mg/dl for cholesterol and 130 mg/dl for LDL. Current research efforts will undoubtedly clarify the cholesterol–heart disease picture within the next two to three years.

Minor Risk Factors That Can Be Changed
Sedentary Lifestyle

Is Exercise an Underestimated Risk Factor?

The great majority of exercise studies suggest that regular exercise significantly reduces the risk of coronary heart disease, and that a sedentary existence is a significant risk factor, quite independent from all the other risk factors.

The first important study on exercise was reported from London in 1953; this study found that conductors on double-decker buses had only 46 percent of the mortality rate from heart disease that was experienced by bus drivers, whose job did not require walking up and down the double-decker bus stairs and who remained seated during the entire working day. The same investigators found that exercise seemed to protect postal delivery workers, who were more active than the relatively sedentary postal clerks. Men who engage in vigorous leisure-time exercise have been reported to have 50 percent fewer heart attacks than their sedentary peers. A study in San Francisco longshoremen found that vigorous physical activity significantly reduced the risk of fatal heart attacks, especially in younger men. Among 16,936 male Harvard graduates, sedentary men were found to have a 64-percent higher risk for heart attacks than their classmates; it is interesting to note that varsity sports participation in college had no protective effect unless the athletic activity was continued in subsequent years. The Framingham study noted that exercise seemed to have a protective effect in men, but not in women.

Because of confusing data that arose from these as well as other studies, in July 1987 the Centers for Disease Control of the United States Public Health Service systematically reviewed all of the available medical literature and located 43 scientifically sound studies that they carefully analyzed. The CDC found that a sedentary lifestyle virtually *doubled* an individual's risk of having a heart attack; this result was similar to the frequency risk for other risk factors, which are 2.1 for uncontrolled high blood pressure, 2.4 for elevated cholesterol, and 2.5 for cigarette smoking.

When these risks are put in the context of the numbers of persons in the U.S. population afflicted with each of the risk factors, an important fact becomes obvious. The estimated national percentage of persons with elevated blood pressure is approximately 25 to 30 percent of the population. Eighteen percent smoke 20 cigarettes per day or more, 36 percent have elevated serum cholesterol, yet 59 *percent* of Americans do not perform regular physical exercise. The statistics suggest that the numbers of persons at risk for developing heart disease because of elevated serum cholesterol, high blood pressure, or cigarette smoking are actually relatively small when compared with the number of persons (144 million) who are at risk because they do not engage in a regular physical exercise program. Therefore, of these four coronary heart disease risk factors, physical activity should no longer be classified as minor; in fact, from a numerical point of view, it affects far more people and therefore appears to be a more important risk factor than the so-called major risk factors.

Effect of Exercise

Exercise training favorably affects risk factors, and careful analysis of studies in thousands of men and women has clearly demonstrated that it significantly reduces the risk of heart disease. A sedentary existence is a major *independent* risk factor, that is, it is independent of the good effects of reducing blood pressure, cholesterol, and triglyceride levels and increasing the level of the "good fat," HDL. Exercise improves metabolic function and contributes substantially to feelings of well-being.

Benefits of Exercise on Weight Reduction

Exercise is an important factor in weight control and in weight-loss programs. An increase in the basal metabolic rate or the metabolism helps to burn body fat. In addition, some scientists have indicated that exercise lowers the "set point," the point "chosen" by a control center in the brain at which it considers the weight to be ideal. This theory suggests that this control center influences the amount of calories eaten and may even metabolically affect the efficiency of calories that are consumed. Exercise may therefore actually help to control rather than increase the appetite by lowering the set point, which senses the active person's needs to be thin (to achieve the proper amount of body fat), and thereby reacts by diminishing the appetite.

Finally, regular exercise helps the body consume fat by building up new muscle tissue. Some specialists in the field recommend weight training as an effective method for developing lean muscle tissue, thereby achieving, with aerobic exercises, the best of all metabolic worlds—muscle increase, fat reduction, weight reduction, and car-diovascular fitness.

Benefits of Exercise on Blood Fats

Dr. Kenneth Cooper, the founder of the Cooper Clinic and director of the Aerobics Center in Dallas, Texas, is an acknowledged world leader in health and fitness; he reported clear-cut evidence (as have other studies, such as the one of postal workers cited earlier) that brisk walking over a period of just a few months would significantly increase the "good fat," the HDL cholesterol levels. Moderate or more vigorous exercise resulted in even more significant increases in HDL levels and it improved cholesterol/HDL ratios in normal patients as well as in heart-attack survivors.

The data clearly demonstrated a direct correlation between fitness, HDL levels, and the cholesterol/HDL ratio, but there was no clear correlation between fitness and total blood cholesterol per se. It further suggested that HDL cholesterol would usually reach a certain level and would not climb higher, no matter how much additional exercise was performed, and that it would decrease significantly if exercise was discontinued. Finally, Dr. Cooper pointed out that there is no age limit on the beneficial impact of aerobic exercise on raising HDL levels.

Other Benefits of Exercise

It has been suggested that exercise has a beneficial effect on high blood pressure, although the evidence is not entirely conclusive. Certainly, many hypertensive individuals are also overweight, and weight loss due to exercise has itself been shown to lower elevated blood pressure significantly.

Osteoporosis, a condition in which bone density is diminished, is a common problem for older adults, especially women; this condition is a major contributor to the more than 1.5 million bone fractures per year. Physical activity, particularly weight-bearing exercises such as walking, will increase bone mineral content and density and/or slow its rate of loss.

A word of caution is necessary; any new exercise program should be started carefully and slowly (see Chapter 11). This is especially important if one plans a program of vigorous exercise or if a self-screening examination (see Chapter 7) indicates the presence of significant risk factors. In the latter instance, a physician should be consulted and an exercise stress test considered. The exercise stress test would be, in essence, a "road test" that determines whether or not exercise can be performed safely and to what level.

Obesity

Obesity, an excess of body fat, should be distinguished from heaviness, which is an excess of body weight. Each of us are made differently (i.e., different size bones and muscles) and, therefore, two people of the same height and weight can have completely different body compositions with total body fat percentages which are miles apart. For example, someone of a light body frame and build can eat too much for his body's build, become obese with a very high percentage of total body fat and still weigh only as much as someone of the same height who is lean but whose muscles and bones are heavier and therefore whose total body fat percentage is normal. A man is considered to be obese if his body fat comprises more than 19 percent (21 percent for women) of his body. Weight is obviously quite simple to measure but precise determination of body fat requires technically sophisticated measuring methods, such as "weighing" a person under water in a large tank or, less accurately, by using special calipers to estimate the percentage of body fat. More recently, simple bioelectrical measurements have been combined with microprocessor analysis devices; these commercially available machines automatically measure the basal metabolic rate as well as the amount and percentages of body fat, body water, and lean body mass. Armed with this information (rather than knowing only the total body weight), a doctor can prescribe an individually designed nutrition, weight reduction and exercise program.

It has been most difficult to determine whether or not obesity is an independent risk factor for coronary artery disease, even though it is frequently associated with other heart-disease risk factors. For example, obese persons are more likely to have higher levels of blood pressure, blood cholesterol, and sugar than leaner persons. HDL levels have been shown to be lower in heavier persons.

Some scientists have considered the possibility that it is not the total body weight (or fat) but the content of the fattening diet that predisposes one to atherosclerosis. Obese persons are motivated to eat by taste rather than by hunger and therefore are more attracted to tasty foods, such as those containing saturated fats, which tend to raise serum cholesterol levels. There seems to be little doubt that people with higher relative weight are more likely to have unfavorable heart-disease-risk-factor status (high cholesterol, high blood pressure, etc.), and that loss of weight improves the risk factors.

Consensus Conference on Obesity

When a medical or public-health issue becomes timely, either because of new scientific developments or because it affects a large percentage of the population, the National Institutes of Health (NIH) organizes a "consensus development conference." These conferences, which began in 1977, bring together biomedical researchers, practicing physicians, and other specialists as well as consumers, representatives of public-interest groups, and other interested individuals, to assess the health issues and evaluate the safety and efficacy of drugs, devices, and procedures.

In the past, most public attention focused on obesity has been devoted to cosmetic and aesthetic concerns about body weight. When it became increasingly obvious that obesity was a serious public-health problem, a National Institutes of Health Consensus Development Conference on the Health Implications of Obesity was convened in February 1985. This issue was obviously extremely important because at least 20 percent of the adults in the United States are overweight.

The conference report concluded that obesity had adverse effects on both health and longevity, and that it was a specific risk factor for the development of coronary artery disease. In addition, it noted that obese patients had a higher incidence of high blood pressure, abnormal blood fat patterns (including higher cholesterol levels), and diabetes. Because obesity was frequently associated with other cardiac risk factors, the total risk to overweight patients was often significantly increased. They concluded that obesity appeared to have a direct relationship with all the other major coronary risk factors other than cigarette smoking, and that weight control was highly desirable in all patients, but especially those with diabetes, hypertension, or elevated levels of cholesterol or triglycerides.

Diabetes Mellitus

Diabetes mellitus (sugar diabetes) is considered to be present when blood sugars are consistently found to be abnormally elevated. Diabetes is usually caused by an inadequate supply of the hormone insulin, which is produced in the pancreas. Insulin helps the body burn sugar and other carbohydrates, and therefore the sugar levels in the bloodstream will climb above normal levels when the pancreas does not produce enough insulin to meet the body's needs.

Diabetic patients tend to develop arteriosclerosis at an earlier age and to have an increased frequency of heart attacks, strokes, and circulation problems. They frequently demonstrate other risk factors such as high blood pressure, elevated serum cholesterol, and obesity. Even when the blood sugar is brought under control with diet, weight reduction, and medications, premature and often silent coronary heart disease still occurs more frequently in diabetic patients than in nondiabetic ones.

Stress and Personality Type

Since stress is present to a greater or lesser degree in us all, let's move on to this "minor" risk factor in the next chapter.

Stress: An Old Problem with a New Meaning

"My life is at the mercy of any scoundrel who chooses to put me in a passion." This wise observation, by the famous eighteenth-century surgeon John Hunter, resulted from his personal observations that stressful events were not infrequently followed by sudden, unexpected death. In 1628, another philosophical physician, William Harvey, accurately concluded that "every affection of the mind that is attended with either pain or pleasure, hope or fear, is the cause of an agitation whose influence extends to the heart."

Stress has always been considered to be a so-called minor heart-disease risk factor; it should be recognized, however, that this categorization may not be accurate since, as with lack of exercise, its contribution may, in fact, be a major one. Carefully controlled scientific studies have been extremely difficult to mount because of problems inherent in measuring the degree and direct effect of stress without influence from other factors such as age, sex, cigarette smoking, and blood cholesterol level. Despite these difficulties, many highly regarded research studies have carefully analyzed the relationship of depression, anxiety, and neuroticism to coronary heart disease. They add support to the growing concept that psychological factors may be extremely important in the precipitation of heart attacks and sudden death, events occurring frequently in persons who suffer failure, frustration, intense disappointment, or recent bereavement, or who possess certain personality and behavioral characteristics. Strong evidence now exists that mental stress can significantly reduce coronary artery blood flow, and that such stress frequently precedes the development of symptomatic heart disease.

Emotions and Heart Function

Emotions are experienced both psychologically and physiologically. Although the subtleties of psychological expressions (e.g., anger, fear, anxiety, joy) are richly varied, the body's repertoire of physiological responses is, to the best of our knowledge, relatively limited. Emotional arousal results in stimulation of various parts of the nervous system, which can affect the heart and blood vessels either directly or through the actions of hormones that may be produced in response to these stimuli. The effects produced are similar to those that follow physical stress or exercise; that is, increases occur in heart rate, blood pressure, oxygen consumption, heart blood output, and resistance of blood flow in the fingertips. In addition, the heart's need for oxygen is increased and, most important, the heart may become more irritable, rendering it susceptible to malfunctions of rhythm, including ventricular fibrillation, the usual cause of sudden death. Emotional stress and traumatic life events frequently occur prior to acute heart attacks, arrhythmias, or sudden death, and therefore appear to be capable of producing physiological and biochemical events in the body that can cause these cardiac catastrophes.

Stress and the Immune System

Relatively recent research has demonstrated that stress influences brain activity by causing several sections of the brain to produce hormones and chemical "messengers" called *neurotransmitters*, which travel throughout the body to the heart, muscles, endocrine glands, and immune system. Research in this area has been stimulated recently by the intense scientific effort to find a cure for AIDS.

The hormones produced by the adrenal glands (cortisone and adrenaline, or epinephrine) seem to affect immune cells directly, sometimes enhancing their effectiveness and sometimes inhibiting it. These hormones (as well as their chemical cousins, such as norepinephrine) have been found to remain elevated for surprisingly long periods when someone is not able to relax or unwind after extremely stressful experiences or after work. The nature of the exact link between stress, the immune system and disease is not entirely clear. It is quite possible that prolonged stress alters the immune system (making the body more susceptible to infectious diseases) and the body's biochemistry, and could have profound, long-lasting effects on the cardiovascular system.

Effect of Occupation

In any review of the long list of psychologically stressful events, separation and/or divorce always tops the list as being the most stressful because of their prolonged nature, with inadequate job gratification being a close second. Psychosocial factors associated with occupation have frequently been implicated in the development and progression of cardiovascular disease; these factors include stress related to a particular job, forced change, and unemployment or retirement. An individual who is content and happy with his occupation can work many and long hours feeling well and without untoward effects on the cardiovascular system, whereas even one or two hours of distasteful and ungratifying work can be too much for anyone, let alone a heart patient who hates his job. Therefore, even patients who have suffered severe heart attacks can usually return to their jobs, even if the hours are extremely long, if they (1) enjoy their work, (2) are not overly competitive in their work activities, and (3) are able to learn simple methods for coping with the unavoidable daily stresses that are likely to occur in any occupation (see Figure 11).

MOST DIFFICULT JOBS (Responsibility— No Control)	WARNINGS	COPING
Inner-city high school teacher	Palpitations	Relax
	Stomach pains	Maintain humor
Police officer	Insomnia	Meditate
Miner	Headaches	Exercise regularly
Air-traffic controller	Persistent fatigue	Eat sensibly
Medical intern	Irritability	Get a massage
Stockbroker	Nail biting	Limit alcohol,
Journalist	Lack of concen-	coffee, tea
Customer service/ complaint depart- ment	tration	Take comfort with friends/family
	Increased use of alcohol and drugs	Fight back
Waitress	Hunger for sweets	Delegate respon-
Secretary	Frequent illness	sibility
		Confront boss
		Resign job

Figure 11. Who's stressed, how to tell, what to do about it.

The most difficult jobs are those with a great deal of responsibility but with minimal personal control (police officer, inner-city high school teacher, traffic controller, miner). Symptoms associated with stress include palpitations, insomnia, headaches, persistent fatigue, irritability, lack of concentration, and chest pain or abdominal pains. Stressful situations frequently also lead to increased drug and alcohol consumption.

Life is a problem-solving exercise, and as a result, stress is *potentially* present at all times; if one is adept at problem-solving, the untoward effects of stress are minimized. It is therefore not simply the presence of a particular stress but rather one's reaction to it that really counts. For example, a taxi driver in the streets of New York City performs his task without concern or thought, but put a physician, politician, or a corporate executive behind the wheel of his cab, and you can imagine the stress in that situation. And reverse the roles; consider how the cabdriver would be lost and emotionally stressed if he suddenly found himself at the head of the table in a corporate boardroom. The ability to cope with job insecurity, tyrannical bosses, and occupationally related physical or psychological trauma of any form is necessary in order to be successful at any job, but is especially necessary in those occupations that carry a lot of responsibility but little power (again, see Figure 11).

"Type A" Behavior

Stress has been categorized in many ways; one classification distinguishes stress related to intense behavioral activities, the so-called Type A behavior. Type A behavior has been carefully evaluated over the past 30 years as a possible risk factor for coronary heart disease. It has been characterized as occurring in persons with relatively high levels of aggressiveness, hostility, ambition, and competitive drive associated with a chronic sense of urgency in daily activities. Type B persons are those not afflicted with Type A behavioral manifestations; they tend to be more passive, less disturbed by environmental stress, and less involved in the urgency of time.

"Type A" Risk

Some research studies have found Type A men under the age of 55 to have over twice the prevalence of coronary heart disease when compared to similar groups of Type B men. Interestingly, this relationship appeared to be insignificant for men over the age of 55, but was found to be much stronger in white-collar workers than in blue-collar ones, and in women. These studies concluded that Type A behavior had the same risk-factor strength as cigarette smoking, elevated blood pressure, and serum cholesterol.

More recently, however, the positive relationship between Type A behavior and coronary heart disease has been challenged and found not to correlate well with the risk of recurrent heart attacks or the coronary death rate. In January 1988, a major study published in the *New England Journal of Medicine* concluded that the death rate was *lower* in patients who had previously suffered a heart attack if they had Type A rather than Type B personalities; in fact, the data went so far as to demonstrate that the Type A personality structure actually appeared to protect people from dying rather than make them more vulnerable.

The early, impressive indications that Type A behavior was an independent risk factor for coronary heart disease is now regarded as misleading by many scientists who work in this field. The character of the stresses that influence the development of symptomatic coronary artery disease appear to be far more complex than was previously thought, and cannot therefore be divided simply into Type A and Type B categories. As a result, many scientists are slowly drifting away from the preoccupation with Type A behavior. Current research is unearthing evidence that psychological states such as depression and hostility may generate much more increased cardiovascular risk than does simple Type A behavior.

Type A personalities who enjoy their work and their lives, and who are productive, conscientious, and *not competitive*, are probably at the same or lower risk of developing heart problems than are many of their more "relaxed" Type B counterparts, assuming that all of the other risk factors are the same.

Stress and Sudden Death

The recent consensus that Type A behavior plays a different role in the complex psychological picture of coronary heart disease than previously thought seems to confirm studies that have been performed for many years on sudden death occurring during or soon after psychological stress. One interesting paper reviewed the scientific literature and 170 press reports of sudden death occurring over a six-month period; life circumstances that were alleged to have precipitated the sudden deaths were then carefully identified and classified. The author identified eight specific categories of life circumstances that often precede sudden death:

1. Collapse or death of a close friend or relative
2. Threat of loss of a close person
3. Acute grief
4. Mourning or the anniversary of a loss of a close person
5. Loss of status or self-esteem
6. Personal danger or threat of injury
7. The period after the danger is over
8. Reunion, triumph, or happy ending

In all of the reported circumstances, the sudden-death victims were involved in events that were impossible to ignore and to which their response was either overwhelming excitation or surrender, or both. The study concluded that a combination of reactive psychological responses to one or more of these life circumstances produced neurological effects including the classic "flight or fight" response, which, in susceptible individuals, may have been directly responsible for their sudden deaths.

If psychological stress is indeed a factor that potentially contributes to sudden death in a vulnerable or at-risk population, identification (by careful evaluation of their psychiatric makeup and understanding of the emotional and physical mechanisms involved) of the patients who are at risk will almost certainly reduce the incidence of sudden death, since these very understandings will permit appropriate drug and/or psychological intervention.

Stress and Coronary Artery Blood Flow

Recent studies have assessed the relationship between acute mental stress and reduced coronary artery blood flow (myocardial ischemia). As noted in Chapter 2, the transient myocardial ischemia that is frequently observed in patients even with known coronary artery disease commonly occurs without symptoms, at low heart rates, and follows a circadian pattern. Mental stress, like physical stress, can be associated with, and frequently appears to be responsible for, the production of both painful and pain-free decreases in coronary artery blood flow.

A recent paper published in the *New England Journal of Medicine* clearly demonstrates that a variety of mental stresses can cause episodes of myocardial ischemia in patients who already have diseased coronary arteries. The magnitude of abnormalities produced by the most potent mental stress was similar to that induced by vigorous exercise in the same patients. These findings confirmed previous Holter monitoring studies, which suggested that transient episodes of inadequate blood flow in the coronary arteries occurred more frequently during periods of mental stress. The similar characteristics observed during ambulatory Holter monitoring and laboratory-induced mental stress were striking: during both, the ischemia was predominantly pain-free and occurred at heart rates well below those noted during exercise testing that resulted in ischemia. Therefore, the ischemia apparently occurred because of a reduced oxygen supply due to coronary artery spasm as a result of the mental stress, and was minimally, or not at all, the result of other factors, such as increased heart rate. The *New England Journal of Medicine* study concluded that a causal relationship existed between acute mental stress and inadequate coronary artery blood flow, usually occurring without any pain, in patients with coronary artery disease.

Conclusion

The Committee on Stress, Strain and Heart Disease of the American Heart Association has labored for years in an attempt to determine the effects of stress on coronary artery heart disease. The last official pronouncement of this committee was published in May 1977, at which time it noted that continued emotional stress to which an individual may be subjected over months or years may contribute to the progression of arteriosclerotic heart disease, but strong scientific data to support the relationship was not present at that time.

In July 1987, the American Heart Association sponsored a major symposium in which many papers were presented on the effects of stress in coronary artery disease, hypertension, and sudden death. The study group reporting on the effects of chronic or long-lasting stress on coronary heart disease concluded that the responses of individuals to stressful challenges in their social environments, when combined in the right way with the individual personality characteristics of the persons themselves, would "promote lesion development in the coronary arteries and aorta." In other words, the American Heart Association's task force at this meeting concluded that although the scientific evidence was not overwhelmingly convincing, there were innumerable studies that demonstrated the strong association between chronic stress and the development of coronary heart disease.

Stress is one of the risk factors that will be factored into the self-screening test that follows in the next chapter. Self-screening is the vital first step in the process of preventing the development (or worsening) of a heart problem—or sudden death.

7

Self-Screening and Recommendations for Diagnostic Testing in 1989

Certainly there are no medical controversies regarding which diagnostic techniques doctors should use in patients with previously diagnosed heart disease (heart attacks, angina, congestive failure, etc.). There are no issues, no questions; we know exactly what to do and which diagnostic tests are needed for each category of patient.

But there is still a great deal of controversy about how to find and help the symptom-free patient, those individuals who form the submerged mass of the iceberg. What techniques and methods shall we use, and when shall we use them? Remember that silent myocardial ischemia may result from coronary artery narrowing or blockage, coronary artery spasm, clotting of blood elements, or a combination of any or all of these factors; or it may occur because of a basic defect in the body's pain-appreciation mechanism. The approach to finding patients afflicted with SMI will vary depending upon the screening history and the results of both the physical examination and laboratory tests.

The Totally Asymptomatic Patient

It is obviously quite impossible and, in fact, quite inappropriate to subject *all* symptom-free people even to standard treadmill stress tests, let alone thallium stress tests and/or coronary arteriograms.

Instead, we attempt to identify an "enriched" population, that is, a smaller group of patients who are more likely to have abnormal diagnostic tests caused by unsuspected heart disease, even though they are totally without symptoms. Screening all patients in a step-by-step fashion will identify patients afflicted with SMI, and also achieve certain health benefits unrelated to SMI, such as detecting patients with high blood pressure, elevated serum cholesterol, and silent heart attacks.

Cholesterol Screening

The National Heart, Lung and Blood Institute of the National Institutes of Health and the American Heart Association have recommended that *all* adults over the age of 20 be screened with a simple blood cholesterol determination (see Figure 12) and, if necessary, with a study of the other blood fats. In addition, some authorities have strongly suggested that all children whose parents have high cholesterol levels or a history of coronary artery disease should be screened.

Cardiovascular Screening

Cardiovascular screening currently is recommended for all men starting at age 40 and for women at age 50 or at the age of menopause. Screening should also be considered for men below the age of 40 or women below the age of 50 under certain conditions that will be described below.

Patient Self-Screening

Men and women of any age should screen themselves as is graphically demonstrated in Figure 13, but first, the following Sudden Death and SMI Risk Factor Profile should be completed. This simple questionnaire will start you on the path to avoiding coronary heart disease by alerting you to the presence of significant risk factors.

Self-Screening: Sudden Death and SMI Risk Factor Profile

MAJOR FACTORS	YES	NO
I have symptoms of chest pain	____	____
My cholesterol is high (over 200 mg/dl)	____	____
My blood pressure is high (over 140/90 mm Hg)	____	____
I smoke cigarettes	____	____
My parent(s), sister, brother, died of coronary heart disease before age 60	____	____

OTHER FACTORS		
I am a male	____	____
I am under a great deal of stress	____	____
I am overweight	____	____
I do not exercise regularly	____	____

Self-screening will help you determine whether you should consult a physician immediately or whether you should attempt to improve abnormal risk factors by yourself.

With Symptoms

If you have symptoms of pains in the chest, back, teeth, jaws, neck, abdomen, or upper extremities, or if you have other symptoms such as fatigue, weakness, indigestion, palpitations, breathlessness, or any unexplained, prolonged symptom involving the abdomen, chest, back, or upper extremities, you should consult your physician. You should do so *regardless* of your age and your answers to the remainder of the self-screening questionnaire.

Without Symptoms

On the other hand, if you have no symptoms, select the chart (figures 12–18) that is correct for your sex and age. If you have a family history positive for coronary artery disease (defined as a family history in which one parent or sibling under the age of 60 has or has had symptoms of coronary artery disease or has suffered a heart attack, sudden death, etc.), high blood pressure exceeding 140/90 (although some scientists place the cutoff point slightly higher, at 160/95), or elevated blood cholesterol (over 200 mg/dl), you should consult a physician regardless of your sex and age. The physician should lead you through the various testing phases as described below.

If you have no symptoms and *do not* have a positive family history, high blood pressure, or elevated serum cholesterol, you should attempt to control stress, lose weight if needed, discontinue cigarette smoking, and initiate a regular exercise program; if you are unsuccessful in any or all of these efforts, it is mandatory for you to consult your physician and seek his help.

One final word of caution: If you plan to enter a vigorous exercise program, it would be wise to see your physician and obtain a treadmill exercise stress test to determine how much exercise you can perform safely. The treadmill stress test, as well as all of the other advanced testing procedures, will be discussed in detail in Chapter 10.

Doctor Screening of Symptom-Free Patients

Are Important Risk Factors Present?

The doctor should screen patients of all ages in order to help him decide whether further testing is needed. He should obtain a careful and complete history focused on cardiac-risk-factor analysis and then perform a full physical examination. As indicated previously, men are at greater risk than women (especially premenopausal women), and the four most important risk factors that, if present, will place patients in the high risk category for coronary events include:

- Positive cigarette smoking history
- Elevated blood pressure
- A family history of early heart disease
- An abnormal blood lipid profile in which the total cholesterol is elevated above 200 mg/dl, or the LDL (low-density lipoproteins) is over 130 mg/dl.

CHOLESTEROL SELF-SCREENING

MEN AND WOMEN OF ANY AGE

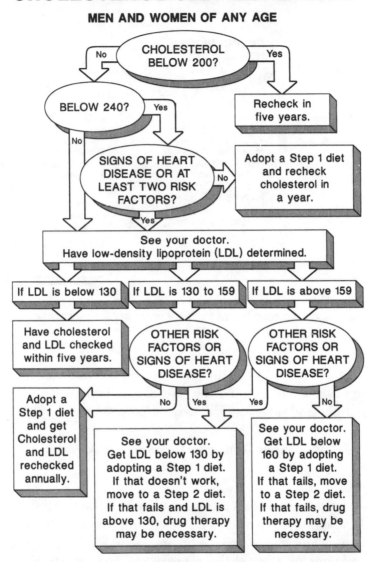

Figure 12.   This chart demonstrates how men and women of any age should screen themselves for cholesterol. The American Heart Association Step 1 diet is recommended for the general public. The Step 2 diet more rigidly restricts cholesterol and saturated fat intake.

SELF-SCREENING

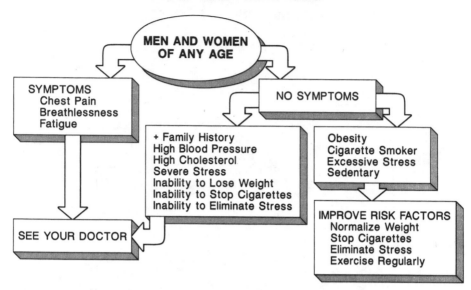

Figure 13.   This chart demonstrates how men and women of any age
should screen themselves for coronary artery heart disease.

Other risk factors that in the past have been considered to be much less significant (but may not be) are excess body weight, diabetes, unusual physical or emotional stress, and a sedentary lifestyle.

Advanced Testing to Determine Risk Factors

Conservative cardiologists recommend more advanced testing for any patient who is older than 40 years of age and possesses two or more of the primary four risk factors, or for anyone older than 50 years of age with only one or more of the primary risk factors. More aggressive cardiologists recommend advanced testing for *all* patients, regardless of age, who have one or more of the four major risk factors, who want to participate in a strenuous exercise program, or who are involved in public transportation operations, such as airline pilots or bus drivers.

DOCTOR'S SCREEN

NO SYMPTOMS

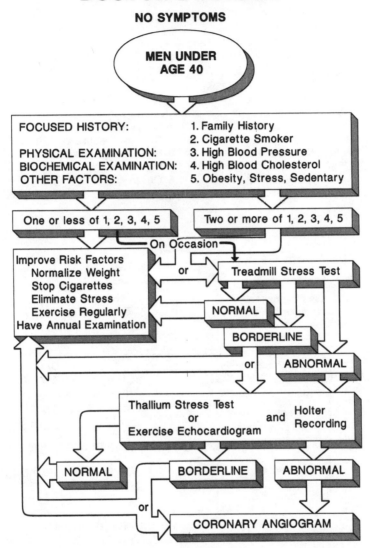

Figure 14. This chart demonstrates how a physician should screen asymptomatic men under the age of 40 for coronary artery heart disease.

DOCTOR'S SCREEN

NO SYMPTOMS

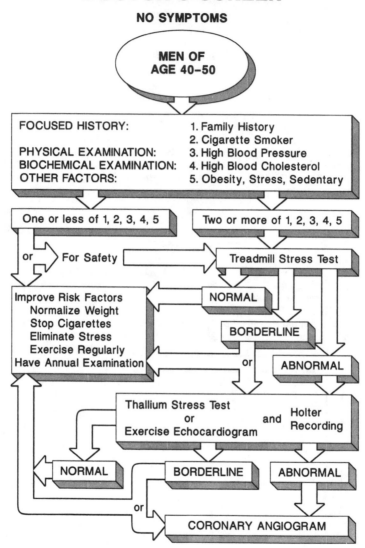

Figure 15. This chart demonstrates how a physician should screen men of ages 40–50 for coronary artery heart disease.

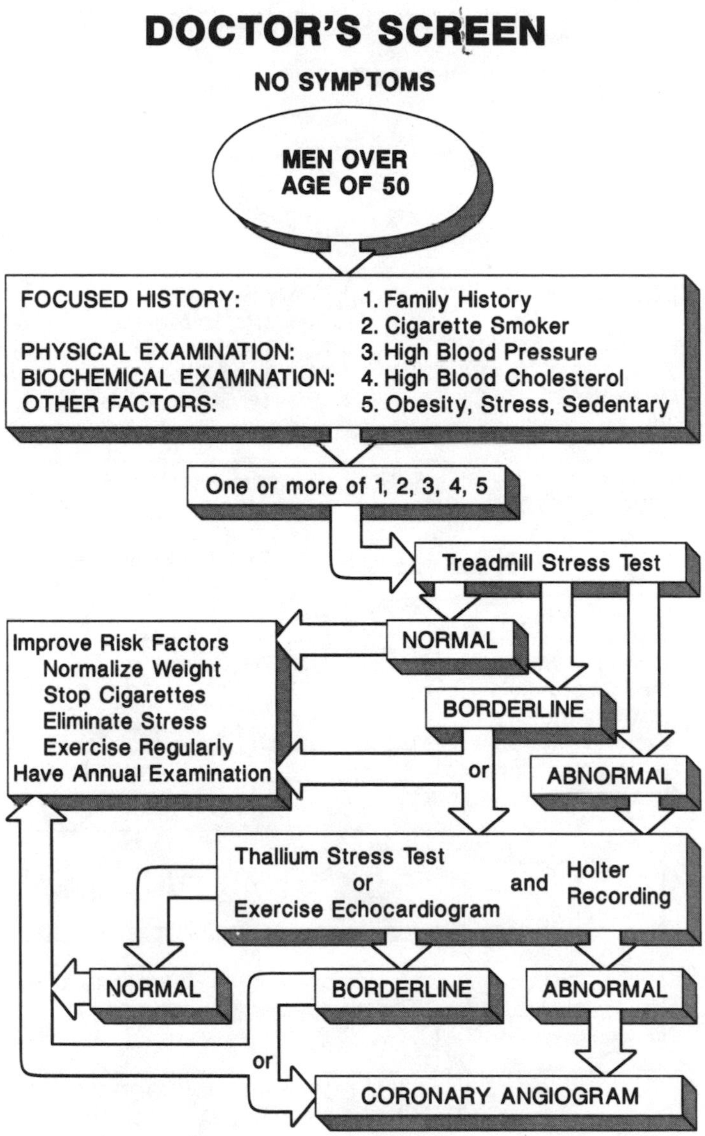

DOCTOR'S SCREEN

NO SYMPTOMS

Figure 16. This chart demonstrates how a physician should screen asymptomatic men over the age of 50 for coronary artery heart disease.

DOCTOR'S SCREEN

NO SYMPTOMS

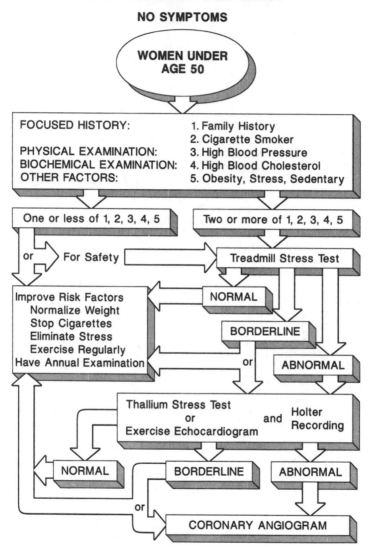

Figure 17.   This chart demonstrates how a physician should screen
asymptomatic women under the age of 50 for coronary artery
heart disease.

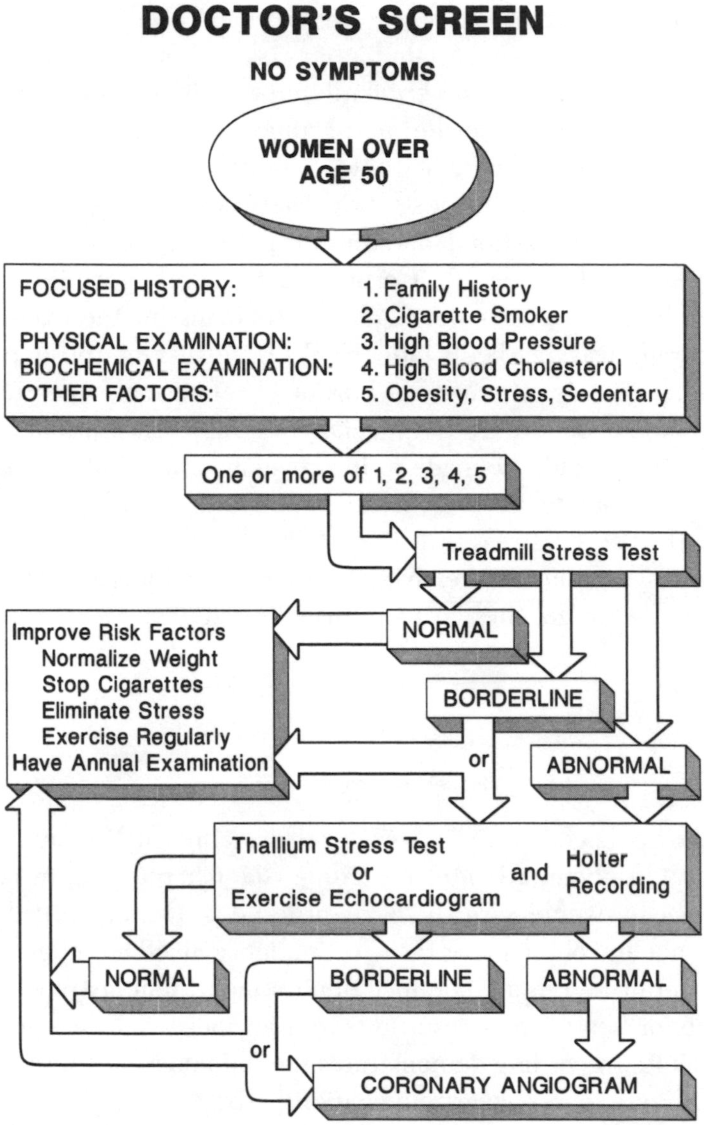

DOCTOR'S SCREEN

NO SYMPTOMS

Figure 18. This chart demonstrates how a physician should screen asymptomatic women over the age of 50 for coronary artery heart disease.

The initial advanced testing procedure normally used is the tread-mill stress test, although, in certain higher-risk patients, the *thallium stress test* or *exercise echocardiogram* might be recommended first. If the standard stress test is borderline or abnormal, a thallium stress test or exercise echocardiogram would definitely be recommended next; however, some cardiologists skip these studies and proceed directly to the catheterization laboratory for performance of *coronary arteriography* (see Chapter 10). Coronary arteriography would defi-nitely be indicated if either the thallium stress test or the exercise echocardiogram was markedly abnormal. If results of these pre-liminary tests are only minimally or borderline abnormal, a coronary angiogram might be ordered (especially in high-risk patients); a vigorous attempt should be made to improve any abnormal coronary risk factors that may be present, and the patient should be retested with one of the various stress tests in six to twelve months or earlier if he develops symptoms suggestive of progressive blockage of the coronary arteries (e.g., chest pain, unusual fatigue).

Holter Recording

If any of the advanced testing procedures are abnormal, many car-diologists would obtain a Holter recording (see Chapter 10); in fact, many physicians would already have ordered a Holter recording whether or not any of the other tests were abnormal. Remember, the stress test performed in a laboratory environment demonstrates the EKG effects of heart stress resulting from an increased heart rate, whereas a Holter recording demonstrates the influence of drugs (e.g., stimulants, tranquilizers, heart medications), stress and ordinary liv-ing activities (work, sleeping, exercise, etc.) on the electrocardio-gram, and therefore, presumably, on coronary arterial blood flow.

Doctor Screening of Patients with High Probability of Coronary Artery Disease

The screening approach to patients with a high probability of coronary artery disease is obviously quite different from that which is used for those individuals who are totally symptom-free. This category of patients includes individuals with typical angina pectoris, those who might have previously suffered a heart attack, or those who have angiographically proven coronary artery disease without having suffered a previous heart attack. These patients are quite frequently symptomatic, but it must again be emphasized that episodes of symptom-free ischemia are three times more frequent than are the painful episodes of ischemia. Screening examinations on these individuals should include a history, a physical examination, and the standard exercise stress test. In many cases, a thallium stress test, stress echocardiogram, and Holter recording are employed. Coronary arteriography may be required intermittently in some patients to determine the progression of anatomical narrowing or blockage of the coronary arteries, or to evaluate the blood flow through previously placed coronary artery bypass grafts.

Doctor Screening of Patients Who Have Previously Suffered a Heart Attack

It is necessary to determine the degree of silent ischemia in patients who have previously suffered a myocardial infarction or heart attack, since the prognosis or long-term outlook appears to be dependent upon the degree and intensity of SMI, and upon its therapy. Evaluation of exercise tolerance (with a treadmill test) and SMI in these patients is also important in determining the degree of physical activity that can be performed safely, and to help guide therapy.

Relatively soon after a heart attack, patients usually will be subjected to a special kind of treadmill stress test (see Chapter 10) known as a "low level" stress test, in which only a minimal to moderate amount of exercise is performed. Quite commonly, this test is performed within one to two weeks after an acute heart attack, before the patient leaves the hospital. If a marked abnormality is detected on the low-level stress test, the cardiologist will frequently recommend coronary arteriography for further evaluation. If the test is negative, borderline, or demonstrates only minimal abnormalities, the physician will usually prescribe medical therapy and follow the patient's progress with periodic stress testing; however, on occasion, a thallium exercise stress test, an exercise echocardiogram, a Holter recording, and/or coronary angiography will be recommended. Routine maximal-exercise stress tests are also performed on heart-attack patients on a regular basis after they have fully recovered from the effects of their heart injury, usually starting three to twelve months after leaving the hospital.

Other Tests

New screening and diagnostic tests will almost certainly be available in the relatively near future for the study of all categories of patients: those with or without known heart disease, those who have had previous heart attacks, angina patients, and so on. Some of these bright stars on the medical horizon are just beyond our line of sight, soon to be here, but others are already here and will be discussed in detail in Chapter 10.

C H A P T E R

The Magnificent Pump: What Goes Wrong?

If all of the blood vessels in our body, big and small, were laid end to end, the resulting tube would be an incredible *12,400 miles* long. Every diagnostic and therapeutic tool in the field of cardiology is dedicated to preserving the ability of the heart to function efficiently as the main element of a simple system that effectively pumps blood through this long tube; this is the heart's only purpose, it has no other role.

The Heart's Chambers: How They Work

The heart is a hollow, muscular, four-chambered organ, about the size of an adult fist, that weighs less than one pound. It lies slightly to the left of the middle of the chest and is protected by the breastbone and the ribs.

The major pumping chamber of the heart, the *left ventricle*, is a thick-walled compartment that delivers blood into one end of the long blood vessel tube with sufficient pressure to pump the fluid along its entire length (see Figure 19). After the oxygen and nutrients carried in the blood have been removed by the various organs and tissues located along the length of the arterial system, the blood is returned at extremely low pressure, via the venous system, to the *right atrium*, the lower collecting chamber on the right side of the heart. It next goes through the *tricuspid valve* to the relatively thin-walled *right ventricle*, which then gently ejects the blood, still under relatively low pressure, across the *pulmonic valve* into the lungs.

The 300 million air sacs located in the lungs "enrich" the blood with oxygen obtained from the air we breathe. Simultaneously, carbon dioxide gas is removed from the blood and exhaled into the air. The oxygen-enriched blood then moves, still under relatively low pressure, into the lower collecting chamber of the left side of the heart, the *left atrium*. It next goes through the *mitral valve* (the one that is frequently affected in patients with rheumatic heart disease) into the workhorse of the heart, the upper left chamber called the left ventricle. The internal pressure in the left ventricle increases dramatically and then, approximately once each second, this extremely strong and efficient chamber ejects the blood forcefully out of the heart, across the *aortic valve*, into the *aorta*, the body's main artery.

After the right and left coronary arteries branch off the aorta at its very beginning, it divides first into a few major arteries, next into many medium-sized arteries, and finally into thousands of smaller and smaller arteries that transport the blood to every part of the body. Each of the smallest blood vessels, called *arterioles*, gives rise to a network of even smaller blood-carrying tubes known as *capillaries*, which reach out to nourish the tiny tissue cells themselves. The thin walls of the capillaries permit oxygen and nutrients to be absorbed by the cells and tissues and, in turn, allow waste products from the cells to pass into the capillaries and then to be carried back to the heart by the venous system and next transported to the lungs and kidneys for proper disposal.

The four heart valves (aortic, pulmonic, mitral, and tricuspid) normally allow blood to flow in only one direction, without backflow or leakage. When leakage does occur as a result of injury or disease (rheumatic heart disease, infections, etc.), the efficiency of the heart as a pump becomes impaired, and permanent damage may result.

In summary, the blood simply circulates like water in a fountain, within a closed circuit. The water is pumped out of the top of the

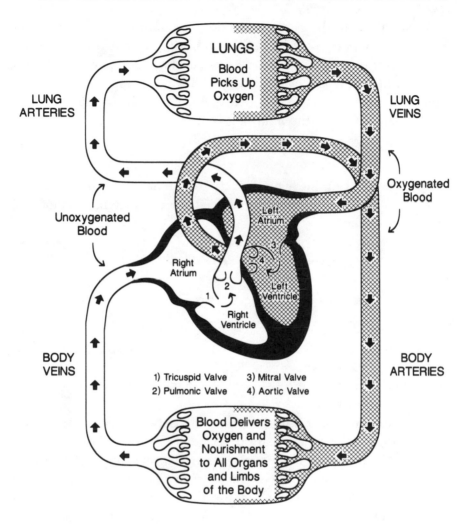

Figure 19.   What the heart does.

fountain, flows to the bottom, and then is pumped under high pressure to spray once again out of the top. Simple, but remember, no pump of equal capacity devised by man has *ever* performed with similar efficiency, longevity, and reliability, which is why the multitude of artificial hearts developed thus far have been relatively unsuccessful. Consider the following facts:

- The normal heart beats between 87,000 and 144,000 times per day.
- During the average lifetime, the heart will beat over 2.5 billion times, moving well over 50 million gallons of blood.
- The 2,000 gallons of blood pumped daily are fully recirculated every 10 to 15 seconds.

The Heart's Circulation: The Coronary Arteries

The heart is like all other organs—it too must receive fresh, oxygenated blood filled with life-giving nutrients if it is to survive and to continue its vigorous pumping activities. The coronary arteries constitute the heart's superb personal circulatory system that nourishes this miraculous pump.

The word *coronary* is derived from the Latin word *corona*, meaning "crown," which pictorially describes the arrangement of these arteries on the surface of the heart, taking a form somewhat similar to a crown atop a king's head (see Figure 5 in Chapter 2). They are the very first arteries that branch off the aorta as it receives blood from the left ventricle. The all-important *left coronary artery* nourishes most of the left ventricle, and the *right coronary artery* carries blood to the walls of the right ventricle as well as to the back and the lower surfaces of the heart. Tiny terminal branches called *collateral arteries* connect the circulation between the two sides. These connecting arteries are called into play when the circulation to one side of the heart or the other is diminished. When this occurs, fresh blood can still reach the region of the heart deprived of its usual blood flow through this physiological "back door." This backup system tends to enlarge for the several weeks after a coronary artery is obstructed, and it can even grow large enough to *prevent* another heart attack if a second coronary artery later becomes blocked.

The right coronary artery divides into smaller arteries at a relatively distant location along its path; the left coronary artery, however, *quickly* splits into two major branches, the *left anterior descending artery* and the *left circumflex artery*. *Triple vessel disease* is the term used to describe severe narrowing or blockage of three coronary arteries, usually the left anterior descending, the left circumflex, and the right coronary arteries. When a patient requires five or six grafts during a coronary artery bypass operation, the grafts will usually include replacements for these three vessels as well as two or three of their branches.

Batteries and Wires

The regularity of the heart's pumping action is the result of tiny electric impulses that are self-generated on an average of once every second by the *sinoatrial node,* the pacemaker of the heart. This tiny "battery" automatically generates electric currents that are conducted along a system of "wires" within the heart muscle itself. If the sinoatrial node fails to operate properly, its function is taken up by one of a series of backup "batteries" scattered throughout the heart; they usually are activated only when the heart's primary pacemaker fails or if a malfunction occurs in its electrical conduction system. The pumping chambers are sparked in a carefully timed sequence by the currents generated in the sinoatrial node; the net result is a contraction or "squeezing down" of these chambers in an orderly fashion, at the appropriate time. The blood is forced to flow systematically from the upper chambers (the atria) to the lower chambers (the ventricles), and then into the general circulation, specifically to the lungs from the right ventricle and to the rest of the body from the left ventricle. This harmonious efficiency would be destroyed if a malfunction were to occur in any one or more of the three major regions described above: (1) in the sinoatrial node (the "battery"); (2) in the conducting "wires"; or (3) in the heart muscle itself.

The Total System

Oxygenated blood is pumped from the left ventricle into the coronary arteries that carry the blood over the heart's surface to its most distant regions and then penetrate the heart muscle itself. These indispensable supply lines provide nutrition for all parts of the heart, which normally operates with harmonious efficiency. If the blood flow through the arteries becomes inadequate however, the heart's perfect timing can be affected because of resulting damage to one of its component parts, thereby diminishing or destroying the heart's ability to nourish the various organs of the body, including itself.

Safety Factors in the Heart

Nature has been kind to us in many ways; for example, we have two eyes, two kidneys, two adrenal glands. If we lose one of these, we always have the other to take up the function of its lost partner, and it usually does so quite successfully. Even though we have only one heart, nature has again thoughtfully provided a backup feature, an enormous safety factor. If a significant portion of the heart is lost owing to damage or injury, temporary or permanent, the remaining portion of the heart will usually take on the load and carry on quite nicely, albeit somewhat less efficiently. A heart that has been permanently damaged by a heart attack will frequently last as long and be almost as efficient as a healthy heart unless the damage is extremely large or critically placed; in fact, one can usually get along quite well for many years (or even for a normal life span) if only 5 or 10 percent of the heart has been damaged. If the degree of damage is *very* severe, physical incapacity may result, and frequently the life span will be shortened. Therefore, we do everything we can to preserve the heart, to prevent damage, and, if damage does occur, to limit the size of the injury. The contemporary approach to treatment of an acute heart attack is aggressively dedicated to the prevention of complications and to saving as much heart muscle as is possible.

BUT EVEN BETTER, WHY NOT PREVENT THE HEART ATTACK BEFORE IT OCCURS? THAT'S WHAT THIS BOOK IS ALL ABOUT.

9

The Ischemic Cascade:
Stunning, Hibernating, Recruiting

For many decades, myocardial ischemia was considered to be an all-or-none process. Heart damage was known to occur if the ischemia was prolonged or severe (as in a heart attack), but if it was only transient or brief (as in mild angina or silent myocardial ischemia), the effects on the heart were thought to be minimal in degree and completely reversible; also, it was presumed that after coronary flow had been restored, metabolism and function would rapidly return to normal and heart structure would be preserved. Inadequate coronary artery blood flow was considered to be an event that simply began with chest pain (angina) and ended after the pain had subsided. We now know that, in most instances, angina (and even a heart attack) is the *final* expression of heart disease and not the initial one.

New understanding of the biochemical and physiological effects of reduced coronary artery blood flow has led us to the conclusion that *any* reduction of the usual blood supply to the heart, whether intermittent or prolonged, whether painful or not, is the beginning of a *cascade* of abnormal events.

When the heart is not receiving oxygen-rich blood—that is, when the oxygen *supply* is too little and/or the oxygen *demand* is too high *at any moment* (see Chapter 2), ischemia may occur, either with or without pain. The first response of the oxygen-deprived heart is to malfunction in its pumping action; this malfunction is *not necessarily* followed by electrocardiographic changes or chest pain. Late in the process, and virtually always only after the pumping and electrocardiographic abnormalities have developed, chest discomfort (angina) will occur in a small percentage of instances; more commonly, chest pain does not occur and the ischemia is then called silent myocardial ischemia.

Thus, the ischemic cascade always begins with poor coronary artery blood flow (for the heart's needs at that moment), resulting in heart muscle malfunction, followed, on occasion, by electrocardiographic changes. Finally, in the minority of instances, this series of events culminates in chest pain or discomfort.

Permanent Heart Damage

The concept of the ischemic cascade helps us to understand why completely silent (or, less frequently, painful) episodes of diminished coronary artery blood flow can result in significant injuries to the heart muscle itself that are totally symptom-free and either transient or permanent. These recurrent injuries will eventually diminish the pumping capacity of the heart, whether or not chest discomfort has ever occurred during any of these episodes. Since silent episodes of heart ischemia are at least three times more common than painful ones, and since chest pain is a *late* feature of the ischemic cascade, significant damage to the heart's pumping abilities may occur much before chest pains develop. In other words, by the time patients start to complain of chest pains, they almost always are already afflicted with disturbed heart function of a more intense degree than appears on the surface. Vigorous and effective treatment is therefore absolutely necessary to prevent not just the obvious (i.e., the chest pains), but, *more important,* to stop the ischemic cascade from taking place, to prevent temporary or permanent malfunction of the heart muscle itself, and even to prevent sudden death.

The "Stunned" Heart: Hibernating and Recruiting

As indicated above, it was previously thought that (1) when the heart's oxygen balance was restored before permanent injury (heart attack) occurred, heart function returned *rapidly* to normal, and that (2) when the blood flow to the heart was diminished and prolonged beyond a critical point, irreversible heart damage occurred, as a result of which complete recovery of its pumping function could never be restored. It has now been clearly demonstrated that periods of ischemia, even if too brief to cause heart damage, may nevertheless be associated with profound changes that will result in diminished function of the heart as a pump. This dysfunction has been found to persist for *prolonged* periods—hours, days, or even weeks after the blood flow has been restored. In other words, if a heart is "stunned" by even a brief episode of ischemia, lasting only minutes or hours, prolonged impairment of the pumping ability of the heart may result. Stunning will occur whether or not chest pain is associated with the episode, and therefore, three to four episodes of pain-free stunning occur for every one associated with chest pain.

The Importance of the "Stunned Heart" Concept

Temporary blockage of a coronary artery produces SMI or angina; complete blockage will cause a heart attack with resulting permanent damage of heart muscle. But if the artery is opened quickly (with nitroglycerine, by spontaneous relaxation of coronary artery spasm, by dissolving the clot, or through bypass surgery or angioplasty), before permanent damage occurs, the heart will only be stunned temporarily. It then "hibernates," waiting to recover its function. The duration of the stunning effect is always much longer than the duration of the episode of poor blood flow; if permanent damage has not occurred, return of normal heart function will take place—but only many hours or days after the previously inadequate coronary artery blood flow has been improved. The heart's functional ability will therefore be only temporarily affected, and total recovery will usually be permanent unless the process starts all over again.

If heart stunning occurs *repeatedly* because of recurrent ischemia, whether painful or pain-free, the heart may never have a chance to recover completely, and permanent heart damage will result. Damage may therefore be occurring *silently* in persons afflicted with silent myocardial ischemia. It may also be occurring silently and progressively in patients even with mild angina, which, in the past, has inappropriately been considered by both patients and their doctors to be a minor symptom. Eventually, repeated stunning may result in *ischemic cardiomyopathy*, a condition in which heart function is altered and severe heart failure may occur. Patients with this condition are at greater risk of developing a heart attack or even dying suddenly. Vigorous efforts at treatment, including drug therapy and correction of risk factors and diet, are therefore indicated in order to reduce the incidence of these ischemic episodes and their consequences. Because chest pain is not a reliable indicator of the ischemic cascade, most cardiologists feel that *all* episodes of ischemia, silent or not, should be treated. Only in this way can stunning be avoided. If it does occur, coronary artery flow should be restored as quickly as possible to avoid permanent damage. If the circulation is restored, the stunned heart will "hibernate" and then be "recruited" back to normal function in time.

Summary

1. Inadequate coronary artery blood flow can have four distinct results:
   a. Transient ischemia with or without chest discomfort, electrocardiographic changes, and disturbed heart function. This category includes patients with typical angina.
   b. Severe ischemia causing heart damage and permanent heart dysfunction (a classic heart attack).
   c. Prolonged ischemia, causing heart stunning resulting in abnormal heart pumping activities.
   d. Severe, persistent heart dysfunction, secondary to chronic (days, months, or years); inadequate coronary artery blood flow, but with recoverable function (hibernation).
2. If heart damage has not occurred, heart function can be improved with drugs and/or revascularization (coronary artery bypass surgery, angioplasty, etc.), although the improvement may take weeks or months.
3. In the majority of instances, chest pains do not occur even when the coronary artery blood flow has been critically reduced to the point where either electrocardiographic or profound mechanical pumping abnormalities result. Angina occurs in no more than 25 percent of these episodes, and even less frequently in patients who are diabetic or hypertensive.
4. A malfunction of the pumping activity of the heart occurs first in response to inadequate coronary artery blood flow, followed by electrocardiographic abnormalities, which may then be succeeded, on occasion, by chest pain.
5. Repeated "stunning" of the heart by ischemic episodes, silent or painful, results in permanent damage to the heart. In many instances however, the damage may not

be permanent, the heart may only "hibernate," and function will improve if circulation can be restored.

6. All episodes of ischemia should be vigorously treated to prevent permanent damage. The destructive effects of repeated ischemia can be avoided or diminished in intensity if these episodes, whether painful or silent, can be reduced or eliminated.

In the following chapter we'll see what your doctor should be doing to detect, and then to prevent, the ischemic cascade.

10

What Your Doctor Should Be Doing to Detect SMI

We can launch an effective attack on the invisible enemy, on silent myocardial ischemia or sudden death, only by becoming medical detectives, by carefully looking for clues that will lead to the discovery of cardiac problems long before the onset of significant symptoms.

The Focused Medical History

First, a complete medical history should be obtained by the physician from the patient and/or his family. The physician should focus on the aspects of coronary artery disease that are most likely to alert him to the possibility that his patient is afflicted with symptom-free SMI (or even symptomatic heart problems). The history will detect those individuals at risk for the premature development of coronary insufficiency, those patients who have a higher chance of developing premature coronary artery problems, with or without symptoms.

Risk factors have already been extensively discussed, but some of the information bears highlighting at this time to emphasize the importance of obtaining an adequate heart-oriented history. The history will quickly reveal whether the patient has ever been a cigarette smoker or has a family history of premature coronary artery disease. A significant family history of premature coronary heart disease is obviously important, yet the discovery of a normal family history should not lull the patient or physician into a false sense of security, since this is only one of the important risk factors to be considered. The offspring of parents who lived into their nineties may not be protected from the ravages of coronary heart disease if they smoke two or three packs of cigarettes per day, are obese, have high blood pressure, and/or have moderately or severely elevated serum cholesterol. Whatever good effects are imparted to an individual because of an excellent family history may be nullified if he or she has one or more abnormal risk factors that frequently are avoidable and/or treatable.

Physical Examination

A careful physical examination should be performed to determine whether the patient is obese, is afflicted with vascular hypertension, or has other abnormal cardiovascular findings. The doctor should evaluate the patient's general appearance and look for specific abnormalities that are often found in even totally symptom-free patients. For example, the patient's appearance may give an indication that abnormal thyroid gland function, structural abnormalities of the heart, or congenital abnormalities (such as Marfan's syndrome) are present. A horizontal crease in the earlobe has been reported to be found more frequently in patients with coronary artery disease than in those without this condition. The fundi (i.e., the retinas) of the eyes should be carefully examined since this is the only place in the body where the blood vessels can actually be seen. A routine heart and lung examination can detect abnormalities such as lung congestion, chronic lung disease, heart murmurs, or other heart abnormalities.

Biochemical Studies

A complete blood examination can now be easily performed on everyone, using modern laboratory equipment. For tests that cannot be conducted in the physician's office, he or she may send the blood specimen to a qualified laboratory. A routine examination consists of as many as 24 separate blood tests that will disclose abnormalities in liver or kidney function, identify patients afflicted with diabetes or gout, and evaluate salt and water metabolism of the body. The examination should include a full lipid (fat) examination consisting of serum cholesterol, triglyceride, high-density lipoprotein (HDL), low-density lipoprotein (LDL), and very-low-density lipoprotein (VLDL) determinations (see Chapter 5).

Electrocardiography

Besides being incredibly efficient, the heart muscle is blessed with the strength and durability to pump as many as 140,000 times each day, with only rare extra beats or pauses. Each contraction is fired by a primary "battery" or pacemaker known as the sinoatrial node (see Chapter 8); since the pacemaker occasionally fails, nature has taken the precaution of providing a series of backup pacemakers that become active when the primary one functions improperly.

The normal pacemaker sparks waves of electrical current that travel in an organized and orderly fashion through the heart at the rate of 1,000 mm per second (approximately 22 miles per hour). An electrocardiogram (EKG) is the record of these minute amounts of electricity recorded from the outside of the body. The closer the electrodes (the pickup points) of the device are to the heart itself, the stronger the electrical current, and therefore, all standard electrocardiograms are recorded using electrodes placed across the front of the chest as well as on the arms and legs.

Resting Electrocardiogram

Since Dr. William Einthoven of the University of Leiden in Holland first attached a patient to his huge electricity recorder in 1901, literally billions of electrocardiograms have been carefully correlated with a variety of both functional (e.g., malfunctions of rhythm, pulse formation, or electrical conduction) and anatomical (e.g., heart attacks, chamber enlargement, or valve problems) disorders. The information provided by the electrocardiogram has proven to be invaluable.

The early researchers in electrocardiography quickly recognized the limitations of the standard electrocardiogram; for example, it had to be recorded in a resting state, with the patient lying comfortably on an examination table in the physician's office or laboratory. It soon became clear that the resting electrocardiogram could be completely normal in symptom-free patients even if they were afflicted with profoundly narrowed coronary arteries or even if one or more of the coronary arteries were blocked. In fact, it was quickly recognized that a patient could even be in the earliest throes of a painful *acute* heart attack and that the first electrocardiogram recorded could be completely normal because it was recorded too early in the development of the heart attack. As a result, many physicians have inappropriately reassured these patients and sent them home or back to work; unfortunately, many have left the doctor's offices only to continue in the development of a full-blown acute heart attack—or even to die suddenly that same day.

Treadmill Stress Electrocardiograms

Because of the obvious limitations of the resting electrocardiogram, Dr. Arthur Masters of New York City developed a relatively crude *exercise* stress test almost 40 years ago, known as the "Masters Two Step." In this test, electrocardiograms were recorded before and after the patient walked up and down two wooden steps built to careful specifications. This standardized test was widely used by most cardiologists until approximately 20 years ago, when exercise protocols using stationary bicycles and, later, treadmills came into general use.

The treadmill exercise stress test has proven to be a major step forward in our ability to diagnose causes of chest pains, to predict impending heart attacks, and, more recently, to detect unrecognized, symptom-free, coronary artery disease in the apparently healthy person. It has also proven to be extremely useful in determining the heart's functional capacity in patients who previously have had heart attacks or who have been subjected to procedures such as coronary artery bypass surgery or balloon angioplasty. It is available in the offices of most cardiologists and many primary-care physicians, and in virtually every hospital in the country.

How the Stress Test Is Performed

The physician should carefully outline the reasons for doing the test and should indicate that complications may occur during or after the procedure on rare occasions. Most stress laboratories will then ask the patient to sign a simple informed-consent form for legal purposes.

Food should be avoided for at least several hours prior to the test. Often the subject will be instructed to discontinue certain medications such as beta-blockers and digoxin. Medication should be withheld only upon specific instruction or consent of the attending physician.

Treadmill stress tests have now become quite sophisticated because of advances in computer technology. After electrodes are pasted to the chest, the electrocardiogram and vital signs (such as heart rate and blood pressure) are continuously monitored on video screens, thereby permitting the cardiologist to stop the test if a problem arises in the patient's heart during the procedure. The test should *never* be performed unless a qualified physician is present; he or she should carefully check the patient before, during, and after the exercise and monitor the electrocardiogram, blood pressure, and heart rate *during* the exercise for safety reasons. If these guidelines are followed, the exercise stress test is extraordinarily safe, with complications occurring only rarely. The final results of the test are available for immediate interpretation by the physician upon completion of the study.

Performance of the test is really quite simple. After resting measurements (electrocardiogram, blood pressure readings, etc.) have been obtained, the subject is exercised in a very carefully designed, systematic method. The most widely used exercise program is the Bruce Protocol, in which the motorized treadmill is started at a speed of 1.7 miles per hour and slanted up at a 10-percent grade; every three minutes both the speed and the grade of the treadmill are increased until such time as the physician in attendance ends the test. The doctor will stop the test when a predetermined heart rate (based upon the patient's age) is reached; at this point the stress to which the patient's heart has been subjected is considered to be maximal. The test should be stopped before the maximal heart rate has been achieved if the patient develops abnormal electrocardiographic changes or significant symptoms, such as chest pain, shortness of breath, faintness, or giddiness. This is called a *submaximal stress test*. The average healthy, middle-aged patient will usually be able to exercise for 9 to 12 minutes, but a poorly conditioned, sedentary, elderly individual might be able to exercise for only one or two minutes.

Progressive improvements in exercise technology have made the stress test the best and most reliable noninvasive (i.e., performed without skin puncture or invasion) procedure for the diagnosis of recognized or unrecognized coronary artery disease. It is considered to be a negative test (i.e., significant coronary artery disease is not present) if, after reaching at least 85 percent of the calculated maximal heart rate, significant electrocardiographic abnormalities do not occur at the height of exercise or during the recovery period. However, if the test has to be stopped for any reason (chest pain, fatigue, shortness of breath, etc.) before 85 percent of the calculated maximal heart rate has been achieved, and if the result is negative (abnormalities were *not* detected), one cannot comfortably rule out the presence of coronary artery disease, since the heart rate simply did not get to a high enough level to permit exclusion of the diagnosis with any degree of confidence. If the test is abnormal (positive) at a very low heart rate, the amount of coronary artery narrowing or blockage is usually more severe than it is if the test is abnormal at higher heart rates. Stress test interpretations have improved to the point where physicians are now frequently able to determine with a fair degree of

accuracy the severity and even the location of coronary artery narrowings by careful evaluation of the intensity, timing, and degree of
the electrocardiographic changes that occur during and after completion of the test.

Stress tests are used not only for the *diagnosis* of heart disease but
also to assess the *functional capacity* of the heart. The results guide
the physician in writing his exercise prescription for patients with
known heart disease or who have been subjected to coronary artery
bypass surgery in the past. Over the past decade, it has become
common practice to perform a *low-level* stress test on heart attack
subjects one to three weeks after the injury has occurred. The cardiologist uses this test to determine whether it is safe for the post-
heart-attack patient to engage in the increasingly vigorous physical
activities that are performed during the rehabilitation period without
developing signs or symptoms suggestive of inadequate coronary
artery blood flow and/or dangerous malfunctions of heart rhythm.
Routine or thallium stress testing is also extensively employed weeks,
months, and years after a heart attack to determine, first, the functional
capacity of the heart (its ability to withstand an increased heart rate such
as might occur in stressful or even relatively ordinary activities) and,
second, whether silent myocardial ischemia is present.

Finally, any discussion regarding stress tests would be incomplete
without pointing out that the results of these tests are not always
conclusive. All medical tests have positive (abnormal) and negative
results; *borderline* results, however, occur in a statistically predict-
able fashion, and therefore we classify tests as (1) absolutely positive
(i.e., disease is present), (2) absolutely negative (i.e., disease is not
present), or (3) borderline (i.e., showing possible presence of disease). In a small percentage of patients, tests can also be classified as
falsely positive or falsely negative, but it should be recognized that
our understanding of what is "true" or "false" may change as we
develop more complete information about the natural life history of
any disease process. For example, we now know that many studies
that were once considered "false positive" were not really "false" but,
rather, were true positives in totally symptom-free patients who were

demonstrating the earliest electrocardiographic signs of significant coronary artery narrowing. In any case, it should also be recognized that the treadmill test is accurate in only about 70 to 80 percent of cases for a variety of technical reasons such as case selection, influence of other illnesses, etc. Therefore, many "positive" tests are truly "false positive," occurring in patients who are subsequently found to have absolutely no objective evidence of heart disease, even on angiography (blood vessel X rays; see the subsequent section on nuclear cardiology). But, on the whole, it is an informative and safe test that provides enormous quantities of useful information.

Holter Recording (Prolonged Electrocardiograms)

In the late 1930s, physicist Norman J. Holter began his pioneering studies in the electric potentials of muscles, nerves, and brain waves. The rapid advancements in electronic technology (such as the cathode ray oscilloscope, using the same technology as the TV screen) and techniques developed during World War II enabled him to design a system for sending electrical impulses from the human body through the air to a recorder. He initially transmitted brain waves but by 1949 he was able to also transmit the first electrocardiographic impulses to his radio receiver. Invention of the transistor in 1952 permitted miniaturization of the early transmission equipment, which initially weighed 85 pounds and which Dr. Holter carried in a knapsack that he wore on his back during testing while pedaling a bicycle. The greatest scientific leap forward, however, occurred in the early 1960s, when first animals and then men started to travel out of the earth's atmosphere in space capsules. Their vital functions had to be carefully monitored by radiotelemetry, and later these signals were recorded using newly developed, relatively light, four-pound recording devices that could be carried within the space capsule. The equipment was further modified and refined over the next several years, and by 1966 the first continuous, ten-hour magnetic tape electrocardiographic recorder became generally available for medical use.

Of historical interest are the comments of one cardiologist who, in 1958, objected to Dr. Holter's paper on radio-electrocardiography "on the grounds that there is still so much to be learned and determined with present methods (i.e. orthodox electrocardiography) that adding the fourth dimension of time, with the attendant complication of changing physiology, is not in order." Dr. Holter replied that "it is in the nature of science sometimes to find oneself working on the roof before the second floor is finished and this cannot be helped." Within eight short years, by 1966, Dr. Holter had built the entire house, and soon these bulky and awkward four-pound tape recorders were being strapped onto patients by a small but growing group of believing cardiologists.

Holter recording brought a new dimension to cardiology. Instead of just examining the heart with the standard electrocardiogram for a period of approximately one minute, during which time one might have 60 or 70 heartbeats to review, Holter recording permitted doctors to evaluate ten hours of heart action, during which as many as 60,000 heart beats were recorded. The heart could now be studied in the patient's home or in his working environment, not just in the physician's office or his exercise laboratory. Physicians could now evaluate what effect the stress of ordinary living and working activities had upon heart action and coronary artery blood flow. Technology rapidly improved, and soon it was possible to record a continuous 24 hours of heart activity, producing as many as 140,000 heartbeats for later examination; currently, sophisticated technology permits recording for as long as 120 hours.

The magnetic recording tapes initially used had to be analyzed beat-by-beat in a very labor-intensive fashion, but an alternate method for reading these tapes was quickly developed. The "superimposition" method speeded the tape's journey through the scanning device, requiring only 12 to 24 minutes to analyze a 24-hour tape. Quite recently, user-friendly, self-contained, computerized recording and analyzing systems weighing less than one pound have become available. These devices are simply microprocessors that use computer chips instead of audio tape (on reels or cassettes) and can be worn by the patients for up to five days, providing on-line, real-time summaries of the electrocardiographic activity over these prolonged periods. The results of these studies are rapidly "read" by computers in the doctor's office and are available for his interpretation within minutes.

In 1968, my two partners, Drs. Daniel and Selvyn Bleifer, and I purchased Holter equipment for our practice, and soon we started to receive numerous requests from other cardiologists for studies on their patients. To service these physicians, we organized Cardio-Dynamics Laboratories, the early leader in clinical research in the field of Holter electrocardiography. After conversations with Dr. Holter, we decided that, instead of using the term "dynamic electrocardiography" or "continuous taped electrocardiography," we would call the studies simply "Holter recordings," and the recorders "Holter recorders." Over the next several years we performed literally thousands of studies on patients and analyzed tens of thousands of tapes that were sent to our laboratory from physicians' offices and hospitals in the United States and abroad. We integrated Holter studies into many research protocols concerned with heart drugs that were later approved by the U.S. Food and Drug Administration.

We published our research findings in medical journals and exhibited them at medical meetings. At one of these meetings, the Sixth World Congress of Cardiology, in London in September 1970, we presented a paper titled "Clinical Applications of Dynamic Electrocardiography," in which we indicated that a "prospective study of patients convalescing from myocardial infarction has indicated a high frequency of clinically "silent" ischemic episodes that may have implications in determining activity and drug therapy." This was one of the first descriptions of silent myocardial ischemia. The thousands of American and European physicians at the congress were interested, but distinctly underwhelmed. We were not surprised; they were relatively unfamiliar with long-term ambulatory electrocardiographic monitoring results, since the recorders had been in use in clinical medicine for only two or three years, and in widely scattered medical facilities at that. Relatively few cardiologists were convinced that the procedure was of any value, and even fewer agreed with the concept of silent myocardial ischemia.

Over the next seven years, ambulatory electrocardiographic recording became more widespread and was soon generally accepted by the medical profession and also by patients. Holter recording studies by Drs. Daniel Tzivone and Shlomo Stern in Israel in 1974 suggested that these episodes of poor coronary artery blood flow occurred even during resting activities, during sleep, or when first arising in the morning; these reports were later confirmed by multiple studies both in the United States and abroad, but the majority of cardiologists still did not accept the concept of pain-free ischemia. In 1977, Drs. Steven Schange and Carl Pepine from the University of Florida used this technique to demonstrate that as many as three or four episodes of silent ischemia occurred for every episode of painful ischemia in patients with angina pectoris; this report was politely received, but cardiologists were still simply not ready to accept the fact that significantly reduced blood flow to the heart could occur without pain.

It wasn't until 1983 that a profusion of medical reports started to appear correlating the findings on Holter recording with proven medical diagnostic techniques such as treadmill testing, radioactive isotope studies, and echocardiography. Drs. John Deanfield, Andrew Selwyn, Atillo Maseri, and others at Hammersmith Hospital in London, England, performed some of these studies, which confirmed the results of the Florida studies six years earlier. They found that detailed Holter recordings of angina patients frequently provided a more comprehensive picture of their heart problems than was obtained from the routine examination and electrocardiogram. The subjective symptom of chest pain by itself appeared to be an insensitive indicator of the true frequency of ischemic episodes, since so many of these episodes that were *objectively* demonstrated on the Holter recording were totally pain-free. They noted that many of these periods of poor coronary blood flow were prolonged, that the affected regions of the heart might be disturbed for extremely long periods, and, most important, as indicated above, they confirmed previous studies that indicated that the majority of these episodes were pain-free.

Holter recording has become an indispensable diagnostic tool in identifying and treating many types of coronary heart disease. It appears quite certain that ongoing epidemiological studies will further demonstrate its value in the early detection of unrecognized coronary artery disease. This technique has proven effective in discovering symptom-free heart patients, and because of improving technology and less expensive equipment, screening of the general population will become both practical and fiscally sound in the relatively near future.

Nuclear Cardiology

"Imaging" is a relatively new medical specialty that includes radiology (X ray), sonar studies (echocardiography), MRI (magnetic resonance imaging), and nuclear or radioactive testing. The development of a special camera, known as the *scintillation camera* or *gamma counter*, 20 years ago hastened the dramatic growth that has occurred in the nuclear imaging field.

The nuclear cardiologist is an expert in the use of radioactive substances (radionuclides) in heart studies. These radioactive materials, such as thallium 201 and technetium 99m, tend to accumulate in the heart after they have been injected into the bloodstream. The density of their accumulation is easily measured with the scintillation camera; sophisticated computers are then able to process these measurements and display them in a maplike format for the nuclear cardiologist to study.

Radionuclide imaging has proven to be a safe and effective method for obtaining objective information concerning a variety of heart functions. The tiny amount of nuclear substance used stays in the body for only a short time and virtually never causes a reaction of any kind. The two most frequently used nuclear imaging tests are the *thallium scan* and the *radionuclide ventriculogram* (also called radionuclide angiography, blood-pool scan, or MUGA). These tests accurately measure heart function and coronary artery blood flow, and have been effective in studying the metabolism of the heart muscle itself.

Thallium Stress Test

The thallium exercise stress test is a superb yet simple method for noninvasively measuring the degree and location of blood flow changes in the coronary arteries during and after exercise. When maximum effort is reached during the performance of the standard stress test, a tiny amount of radioactive thallium substance is injected into an arm vein; this material is then transported into the heart itself by the coronary arteries. If the coronary artery circulation in the heart is excellent or good, a significant amount of thallium is detected; if it's bad, the thallium map will outline areas of diminished amounts of thallium, indicating where the coronary flow has been blocked. The results are usually correlated with the standard electrocardiographic stress test, which is performed and analyzed simultaneously with it. The information acquired through these two tests permits the cardiologist to determine indirectly the location and degree of narrowing (or even complete blockage) of any of the coronary arteries, to discover whether the heart has been damaged by a previous heart attack.

Most cardiologists use the standard treadmill stress test as the initial exercise study, since the results are usually quite reliable and are known immediately to both the physician and the patient. However, since the thallium test is really two tests in one (radionuclide and electrocardiographic), it is more accurate than the standard stress test alone. Therefore, from a clinical point of view, if a standard treadmill exercise stress test is borderline or abnormal, a thallium exercise stress test should be performed. This study will provide indirect information regarding the coronary artery circulation that cannot be acquired by other noninvasive techniques at present, although exercise echocardiography (see below) may soon complement or even replace the thallium test.

Radionuclide Ventriculogram

Another radioactive technique frequently used for the evaluation of heart function is the radionuclide ventriculogram (VCG). After red blood cells that have been labeled with the radioactive substance technetium 99m are injected into an arm vein, they travel to the heart, where they are counted by the gamma camera; the acquired information is then processed by specially designed computers. This examination permits the nuclear cardiologist to "see" the pumping chambers; as a result, abnormalities in contraction of one or more of the heart chambers can easily be visualized. Thus far, it has been used only rarely to study patients with unsuspected heart disease, but has been a great help in the evaluation and treatment of patients before and after heart attacks, in drug studies, and to study the effects of exercise and emotion on the heart.

Cardiac Catheterization and Coronary Arteriography

Cardiac catheterization and coronary arteriograms have been performed in this country for the past 30 years and, in the past decade, have become quite routine. Cardiac catheterization permits the radiologist or cardiologist to evaluate the pressures, anatomy, and function of the heart's chambers, and coronary arteriography allows him or her to define the exact anatomy and to determine whether specific narrowings or obstructions of the coronary arteries are present.

The procedure itself is quite simple and is now available in virtually all teaching and university-affiliated hospitals, and in many proprietary hospitals as well. In some centers, two or three angiographic suites function constantly during the day, and are even used quite extensively at night on an emergency basis.

The study is performed on a special X-ray table under sterile conditions; a small area of the skin is cleansed and then injected with a local anesthetic agent similar to the anesthesia administered by dentists. Tiny, pain-free incisions are made either over the artery in the groin or over the one in the front of the elbow; a long, thin, inert plastic tube is then introduced into the artery and advanced to the region of the heart. Its progress is carefully monitored on the X-ray screen by the cardiologist, and even by the patient, who is fully awake, although he or she may be slightly sedated. The flow of small amounts of opaque X-ray dye injected into the various coronary arteries or heart chambers is observed, videotaped, and also recorded on permanent 35-mm motion picture film. Internal chamber pressure measurements are graphically recorded, and the entire procedure is usually completed within 20 to 30 minutes. The patient experiences virtually no discomfort except for occasional, extremely transient feelings of heat or warmth when the dye circulates through the body. Following the procedure, the patient is returned to his or her room, with a pressure dressing over the site of the small incision. Unless a rare problem or complication occurs, or unless the results of the angiogram are extremely abnormal, the patient is usually able to be discharged from the hospital the same day or certainly by the next day.

Coronary arteriography was first performed in 1959. Even at that time the complication rate was relatively small, and it has become even lower because of improved technology and skills; as a result, the indications for performing this procedure have broadened. Cardiologists order this study much more frequently than they did in the past, but only after careful assessment of the complete data in a specific case, including the patient's history, physical examination, and results of all the laboratory tests (treadmill and thallium stress tests, Holter recordings, etc.).

Each patient is completely different from every other, and must be judged individually. For example, coronary angiography might be recommended even for patients with a normal thallium stress test if they have complaints of significant chest pains and/or manifest one or more abnormal major risk factors. On the other hand, a significantly abnormal stress test or thallium study might lead a doctor to recommend coronary arteriography in a totally asymptomatic patient without significant risk factors. Some physicians are much more aggressive than others in recommending this procedure, but neither group is "right" or "wrong" in the borderline cases. Carefully drawn guidelines exist, and therefore, in most instances, coronary arteriography is either clearly indicated or not. A skillful cardiologist can easily guide the patient into making a proper decision, but if the patient remains uncertain as to whether or not the decision is correct, a second opinion should be obtained before going ahead with the procedure.

Echocardiography

Echocardiography is a widely used test that utilizes ultrasound to examine the heart and record information in the form of echoes, that is, reflected sound waves. The echocardiogram is an outgrowth of sonar instrumentation that was initially used during World War II to detect submarines. Over the past 15 to 20 years it has become one of the most important instruments in cardiology for the study of the heart and blood vessels. Technology is improving by leaps and bounds, and usage therefore continues to expand dramatically year after year. In one of its newer applications, it is being used both during and after an exercise stress test to evaluate heart function. "Stress echocardiography" is now complimenting thallium stress studies, and in fact some cardiologists feel that this new use of echocardiography may even replace thallium stress tests as the primary method for noninvasively evaluating the heart's function.

Other Tests

There are a variety of tests that are less frequently used than those previously mentioned, or are in the process of development. These include the following:

Positron-emission Tomography (PET)

Some radionuclides emit *positrons,* nuclear particles that have a positive electrical charge, in contrast to *electrons,* which have a negative electric charge. The PET test uses elaborate and expensive equipment for measuring the actual blood flow through the heart by measuring substances which have been "tagged" with positron-emitting radionuclides. Its use is increasing annually as the equipment becomes available in various major medical centers.

Digital Subtraction Angiography (DSA)

This X-ray study uses advanced computers to improve the quality of angiograms and to study the heart's chambers.

Computer Tomography (CT)

CT scanning of the heart is another computer X-ray technique that is extremely valuable in the diagnosis of anatomical or structural abnormalities of the heart, its surrounding sac (the pericardium), and the great vessels. Recent attempts have been made to use it as a method for studying blood flow through the coronary arteries.

Magnetic Resonance Imaging (MRI)

This method for studying the heart is in a state of flux and evolution at present, and may prove to be one of the major advances in cardiology over the next five years. It does not use X ray or radionuclides, since the images are formed by the resonating effect produced by electromagnetic radiation (radio-frequency waves) on the nuclei of atoms, in this case the atoms in heart tissue. The images are photographed on X-ray film without the use of radiation. This technique is beginning to provide important information regarding the anatomy, function, and tissue characteristics of the heart and its vessels.

Signal-averaged Late Potential (SALP)

The SALP electrocardiogram is a new, computerized test that is being used on both symptomatic and symptom-free patients who are at high risk for developing serious arrhythmias and/or sudden death. Patients who have abnormal SALP studies are usually treated with drugs that will prevent or reduce the incidence of arrhythmias and sudden death.

Electrophysiological Study (EPS)

This study is similar to coronary angiography in that a catheter is inserted into a groin blood vessel and then threaded up into the heart under careful X-ray monitoring. The catheter tip detects the electrical activity of the heart and occasionally is used to stimulate or pace the heart. This technique is now being used extensively in the evaluation of malfunctions of heart rhythms. It provides information that helps the cardiologist to formulate a treatment plan for the *exact* type of arrhythmia that is present. Therapy is particularly important in patients who have significant ventricular arrhythmias (arrhythmias due to irritability of the lower chambers of the heart) such as *paroxysmal ventricular tachycardia* or frequent ventricular *extrasystoles* (premature heartbeats); these rhythm abnormalities commonly are found to be present just prior to the occurrence of the lethal arrhythmia known as *ventricular fibrillation*. EPS studies help us determine which patients are at greatest risk for this rhythm problem, and which drugs will be most effective in its prevention.

The Future in Diagnosis, Treatment, and Life Expectancy

The future is full of promise for improved diagnostic techniques and treatments in the field of cardiology. Space-age technology has already moved into medical therapeutics with the development of the "cool" laser, a beam of concentrated light that is cool enough to remove the sulfurous coating from a match head without igniting it. It may prove to be a major advance in the treatment of vascular disease because of its ability to simply dissolve arteriosclerotic plugs that block the blood flow through arteries, including the coronary arteries. The laser energy is delivered through a flexible fiberoptic tube inside a catheter that is threaded into the artery through a puncture in the patient's skin. It is simple to use this device in leg arteries, but it is still quite difficult to aim the laser beam accurately inside the coronary arteries because of the heart's motion, and therefore the risk of burning through these arteries is quite significant. Efforts are being made to solve this problem by using a more flexible fiberoptic tube that is much smaller—in fact, not much wider than the point of a pencil.

Researchers in a number of hospitals throughout the country are also testing microsurgical instruments that are capable of cleaning out clogged arteries using a rotating blade at the end of a catheter. These devices shear the plaque away from the wall of the artery—a medical Roto-Rooter, so to speak. They are currently being used on the larger arteries of the legs, and are being used experimentally in the coronary arteries.

Experts predict that within a few years lasers and microsurgery will become commonplace and that new drugs will become available for prevention as well as for treatment of heart attack and sudden death. But the hard part of any treatment regimen is in the hands of the patients themselves; they must make every attempt to improve their abnormal risk factors, and that's what the next chapter is all about.

Questions for the Doctor Before a Test

The list of sophisticated tests and procedures grows monthly, and it is therefore virtually impossible for any patient to be fully informed when a specific test is recommended by his physician. Besides being expensive, some of the tests may be uncomfortable, and, most important, significant complications may occur during or following some of these procedures. The patient should therefore thoroughly understand the *ifs*, *ands*, *buts*, *whys*, and *wherefores* of each of these tests; he should understand what information is to be gained, and its importance. He or she should question the doctor about anything that is not clear and have *all* of his questions answered before he approves the performance of the procedure.

Why Is This Test Necessary?

The patient should make certain that he understands why the test is being ordered. Is it necessary to screen for a symptom-free disease or condition, or to rule out a particular diagnosis? Is it being ordered to confirm a possible diagnosis, to assess the severity of a problem, or to determine how well an organ or the body as a whole functions? Is the test being ordered only to reassure the patient that a certain condition is not present?

Is the Test Invasive or Noninvasive? Is It Painful?

Most cardiac tests are completely painless and totally noninvasive, and do not even require anything more than, on occasion, a needle puncture. Invasive procedures such as cardiac catheterization may cause a minimal degree of discomfort because of catheter manipulation, or because the patient frequently must lie quite still for six to eight hours after the procedure is completed. Some hospital-based procedures in very acutely ill patients (such as heart biopsies or removal of fluid from the sac around the heart) may be minimally or moderately uncomfortable, but these procedures usually are absolutely necessary when they are ordered.

Can Complications Occur, and Is There Risk Involved?

Virtually all cardiovascular procedures are risk-free except for the very tiny risks associated with stress tests, coronary angiography, and cardiac catheterization. These risks, although very infrequent, can be extremely profound, and therefore all risks associated with a procedure should be thoroughly discussed with the physician *prior* to the test.

Can the Test Be Delayed?

Delay or avoidance of a diagnostic procedure has its own risks. If progressive coronary artery disease is not diagnosed, treatment will not be started, and major complications such as a heart attack, an arrhythmia, or sudden death may occur. Therefore it is important for the patient to get a very clear statement from the physician spelling out the risk involved in *not* establishing an accurate diagnosis by *not* performing appropriately timely diagnostic tests.

Are There Alternatives?

Is there another test that will give the same information? Why is one test ordered rather than another? What are the cost differences? A careful review of any alternative choices *before* a test is performed is part of medical decision-making for the patient.

Are Office Laboratories Accurate?

Are blood tests performed in the doctor's office or sent out to a commercial laboratory? Does the doctor's in-office laboratory follow the testing procedures recommended by the College of American Pathology (and demanded by some states)? Is the office laboratory certified as accurate by the state? by Medicare?

Many office laboratories are not well regulated or carefully supervised. The tests may be performed by unlicensed, poorly trained technicians on inferior, unstandardized equipment. All medical tests are important. Find out who is doing them, what their qualifications are, and if the equipment is approved and quality-tested on a regular basis.

11

How to Prevent Heart Attacks and Sudden Death: What You Should Be Doing for Yourself

We are no longer ignorant! Having identified the causes and the usual sequence of events in patients with angina pectoris, heart attacks, silent myocardial ischemia, and sudden death, prevention techniques have become obvious. There are common threads linking these heart illnesses, and it is now quite clear how the threads should be woven into a protective approach. Our rapidly expanding base of knowledge has paved the way for prevention of symptomatic coronary artery heart disease, but the patient must do more than cooperate; he or she must take charge actively.

A person can't alter his or her age, sex, or family history, but anyone can improve specific risk factors and lifestyles. Activities or treatments that improve the outlook or prevents the onset of symptom-free silent myocardial ischemia will do the same for symptomatic coronary artery disease and will lower the incidence of sudden death resulting from heart disease. The prevention and treatment of coronary heart disease falls into four broad categories:

1. Specific coronary risk factors should be carefully identified, analyzed, and corrected.
2. Appropriate lifestyle changes should be initiated.
3. New drugs can and should be used for the treatment of symptomatic and symptom-free ischemia, heart attacks, and arrhythmias.

4. Coronary artery blood flow can now be dramatically improved, not only with drugs but also, in selected cases, by performing coronary artery bypass surgery and/or, with increasing frequency, by balloon catheter dilatation (angioplasty).

The next chapter will discuss physician treatment with drugs, surgery, and so on, but in this chapter only the first two items listed above, those issues related to self-treatment, will be covered. Specific benefits will be gained if risk factors are treated; however, the best results can only be achieved if active cooperation on the patient's part is included in the process. It is relatively easy to be given a medicine or to have a specific procedure performed, but it is much more difficult to force yourself to modify your lifestyle or behavior and to follow a prescribed medical regimen. Each patient must acquire the necessary mind-set that will help him or her to follow the prescribed recommendations and achieve the desired results. The doctor's part is easy—to educate. The patient has the hard part—to *do* it.

Correction of Specific Risk Factors

Serum Cholesterol and Obesity: The Diet for a Healthy Heart

Americans have been characterized as one of the most overfed and undernourished populations in the world. Six of the ten leading causes of death in the United States have been linked to diet; these include coronary artery heart disease, high blood pressure, stroke, cirrhosis of the liver, and cancer of the colon and breast. A flurry of governmental pronouncements started to appear in 1979, when the U.S. Surgeon General reported that Americans would be healthier if they consumed less saturated fat and cholesterol. In 1980, and again in 1985, the Department of Health and Human Services and the

Department of Agriculture jointly published their "Nutrition and Your Health: Dietary Guidelines for Americans,"* which again called for avoiding too much fat, saturated fat, and cholesterol. Similar recommendations have been made by the American Heart Association, the American Medical Association, the federally created Inter-Society Commission for Heart Disease Resources, the World Health Organization and other public and private health authorities. The definitive report entitled "The Surgeon General's Report on Nutrition and Health"* was issued by the United States Surgeon General, Dr. C. Everett Koop, in July 1988. This report concluded that more than 34 million Americans have blood cholesterol levels that are too high and that approximately 60 million Americans, or 25 percent of the population, are significantly overweight; he reported that diseases associated with dietary excess and imbalance (coronary artery disease, stroke, high blood pressure, cancer, diabetes, overweight, liver cirrhosis, etc.) touch the lives of most Americans and were responsible for almost 75 percent of the 2.1 million deaths in the United States in 1987.

Poor nutrition is frequently accompanied by obesity; except in the relatively few cases of metabolic abnormalities (e.g., underactive thyroid), obesity is simply the result of consumption of too many calories, of eating the wrong foods. Elevation of blood fats (including cholesterol) is usually contributed to by eating too much fat and cholesterol. Both of these dietary problems can be corrected by improving dietary habits—this seems simple, yet it is difficult for many people to do.

It is obviously important to bring the body weight down to ideal levels (see Figures 20 and 21) regardless of whether the serum cholesterol level is elevated. Abnormal blood fat patterns in obese patients frequently correct themselves as ideal body weight is achieved on a weight reduction regimen; on the other hand, if obese patients are placed on a fat- and cholesterol-controlled diet, weight

*Available through the Superintendent of Documents, U.S. Government Printing Office, Washington, D.C. 20402.

BY HEIGHT

HEIGHT	MEN	WOMEN
ft.–in.	——— lb.	———
4–10	. . .	102–131*
4–11	. . .	103–134
5–0	. . .	104–137
5–1	123–145	106–140
5–2	128–150	108–143
5–3	130–153	111–147
5–4	132–156	114–151
5–5	134–160	117–155
5–6	136–164	120–159
5–7	138–168	123–163
5–8	140–172	126–167
5–9	142–176	129–170
5–10	144–180	132–173
5–11	146–184	135–176
6–0	149–188	138–179
6–1	152–192	. . .
6–2	155–197	. . .
6–3	158–202	. . .
6–4	162–207	. . .

*The weight range is the lower weight for small frame
and the upper weight for large frame. Height without
shoes, weight without clothes.

Figure 20.   Ideal weights for men and women, ages 25–59, based on
insurance actuarial tables. *Source: Statistical Bulletin,
Metropolitan Life Insurance Co., 1983.*

loss will usually occur even as the abnormal blood fat patterns become
corrected.

Permanent reduction in body fat is best achieved in a slow, steady
way. Most health professionals and physicians who are involved in
weight-reduction programs suggest that a true weight loss of no more
than two and a half pounds per week is best; obviously, this isn't as
emotionally gratifying as a weight loss of six or eight pounds per week
achieved on a crash diet, but it is more realistic in terms of a
permanent solution to the problem.

BY AGE

Age(years)	25	35	45	55	65
HEIGHT (ft.–in.)		WEIGHT (in pounds)			
4–10	84–111	92–119	99–127	107–135	115–142
4–11	87–115	95–123	103–131	111–139	119–147
5–0	90–119	98–127	106–135	114–143	123–152
5–1	93–123	101–131	110–140	118–148	127–157
5–2	96–127	105–136	113–144	122–153	131–163
5–3	99–131	108–140	117–149	126–158	135–168
5–4	102–135	112–145	121–154	130–163	140–173
5–5	106–140	115–149	125–159	134–168	144–179
5–6	109–144	119–154	129–164	138–174	148–184
5–7	112–148	122–159	133–169	143–179	153–190
5–8	116–153	126–163	137–174	147–184	158–196
5–9	119–157	130–168	141–179	151–190	162–201
5–10	122–162	134–173	145–184	156–195	167–207
5–11	126–167	137–178	149–190	160–201	172–213
6–0	129–171	141–183	153–195	165–207	177–219
6–1	133–176	145–188	157–200	169–213	182–225
6–2	137–181	149–194	162–206	174–219	187–232
6–3	141–186	153–199	166–212	179–225	192–238
6–4	144–191	157–205	171–218	184–231	197–244

Figure 21. Gerontology Research Center weight tables for men and women, by age. *Source: National Institute on Aging, United States Public Health Service.*

How Many Calories?

Calorie requirement is best calculated by using ideal weight, not the weight in the obese state. A moderately active man who normally weighs 170 pounds requires approximately 2,500 calories to cover his metabolic needs, to keep his weight steady. If he goes on a 1,000-calorie-per-day diet, he will have a deficit of 1,500 calories, and therefore it will take him just over two days to lose a pound of body fat (which occurs when there has been an overall loss of 3,500 calories).

This negative energy balance is best achieved by eating less or by exercising more, although, realistically, it more frequently occurs by eating less. In any case, instead of using a complicated formula to calculate calorie requirements, it is sufficient to say that weight reduction in the average person will almost certainly occur if only 1,000–1,200 calories per day are consumed. An appropriate exercise program (described later in this chapter) will help to achieve a goal of negative energy balance, but for most of us, this goal is best achieved by reducing caloric intake—by eating less.

Refined Sugars

Relatively minor eating modifications will make dieting much easier; however, it is important first to understand several nutritional principles. All carbohydrates are made up of one or more molecules of sugar. Processed or refined sugars are those that have been extracted from their natural sources (such as sugar cane) and, after refining, are used to sweeten foods. These manufactured, processed foods tend to have a high refined-sugar content, often adding calories without providing nutrients or satisfying hunger.

The average American adult consumes one-third of a pound of sugar a day, or 128 pounds a year, accounting for approximately 25 percent of all calories in the usual American diet. The common sources of sugar in the American diet are soft drinks, snacks such as jellies, jams, ices, gelatin desserts, and syrups; milk products such as ice cream, chocolate milk, yogurt, and milk shakes; and pastry, bread, and grain products. Even though sugar contains less than half as many calories per unit weight as do fat products, high-calorie, sugar-rich foods usually come in small packages and as a result, relatively large quantities must be consumed to satisfy hunger. On the other hand, some sugar-containing foods, such as melons, are relatively low in calories per unit weight, and therefore appease hunger with only minimal caloric intake.

Soft drinks that are not low in calories and foods containing refined sugars should be avoided in any calorie-controlled, weight-reduction diet regimen. Alcoholic intake should be only moderate or even totally avoided. An attempt should be made to shift carbohydrate intake away from those foods that are rich in refined sugars, and toward those rich in the food substances known as complex carbohydrates.

Complex Carbohydrates

These substances, frequently called "starches," are made up of branching chains of many sugar molecules. They are found in starchy vegetables including potatoes, rice, corn, dried beans, and peas, as well as in cereals, breads, rice, whole grains, pasta, and a variety of fresh fruits and vegetables. They tend to be *calorically light* when compared to *calorically dense* or heavy foods that are rich in fats and refined sugars (cakes, pastries, etc.). As a rule, complex carbohydrates are extremely low in fat, have no cholesterol, and are generally excellent sources of fiber, vitamins, and minerals.

Complex carbohydrates contain fiber (sometimes called roughage or bulk) such as is found in cereals or bran. Fiber is bulk that helps satisfy the appetite, is not usually absorbed by the digestive tract, and is healthy for a variety of reasons. The best source of complex carbohydrates is oat bran, which has twice the fiber of oatmeal; other sources include grains, dried beans and peas, lentils, vegetables, and fruit. The fiber in oat bran is more soluble than the fiber in wheat bran, and there are substances in oat bran called the "gum fraction" that have a strong cholesterol-lowering effect.

In today's fast-food environment, most carbohydrates come from refined or processed foods such as commercially baked breads and grains, candy, "junk food," and canned vegetables. On the other hand, natural foods consist mostly of complex carbohydrates, and a diet rich in complex carbohydrates is simply not fattening; in fact, it may actually promote weight loss. Complex carbohydrates are among the best foods to eat for weight reduction and control of blood fat patterns, but as with any other food, weight gain will result if these are consumed in excess.

In summary, complex carbohydrates can be filling and provide satisfaction without consumption of excess calories if food intake is carefully planned; however, refined-sugar foods must be consumed in large quantities (and therefore high numbers of calories) to produce a satisfied feeling. Therefore, a major factor in any successful weight-reduction plan is to shift the carbohydrate content of the diet from refined to complex carbohydrates.

Fats and Cholesterol

Fats are necessary components of the body, and function to transport certain nutrients via the blood to the body tissues; they act as energy-storage depots and help to support and protect internal organs. They are ingested in the food we eat and are also manufactured in the body; ingested protein and carbohydrates are among the raw materials used for the manufacture of fat by the liver, which is why eating too much of anything can result in obesity. Obesity can be controlled only by limiting calorie consumption as well as by carefully choosing the types of food consumed. Fat-containing foods are calorically dense and contribute to elevation of serum cholesterol as well as the other blood fats.

The average American ingests between 37 and 41 percent of his or her daily food intake in fat or fat products; per unit weight, these contain over twice the amount of calories as do their protein or carbohydrate counterparts.

- One ounce of high-fat rib roast contains 110 calories, whereas one ounce of low-fat chicken or turkey contains just 49 calories.
- One ounce of high-fat cheese contains 115 calories, whereas one quarter of a cantaloupe contains just 30 calories.

In the average American diet, fat is consumed in the form of red meat (sausage, luncheon meats, hamburgers, hot dogs, roasts, hams, and steaks), dairy products (milk and cheese), commercial bakery products, processed foods (such as macaroni, chili, cheese, canned foods), fast foods (including hamburgers, deep-fried fish, shakes, and french-fried potatoes), and in refined fats and oils used in salads and cooking.

Saturated and Unsaturated Fats

We consume basically three types of fats: *saturated, monounsaturated,* and *polyunsaturated.* A biochemical process called *hydrogenation* determines the degree of saturation of fats. Saturated fats are usually solid at room temperature and are found in foods of animal origin, in dairy products, and in some vegetable oils. They are broken down in the body and tend to increase serum cholesterol to a much higher degree than do monounsaturated or polyunsaturated fats. Therefore, any effective dietary method for lowering blood cholesterol must include reduction in the amount of saturated fats in the diet.

In contrast to animal fats, vegetable fats from plants and trees are all liquid at room temperature, and except for three vegetable oils (coconut, palm, and palm kernel), which are highly saturated, they do not tend to elevate serum cholesterol. Cocoa butter (chocolate) is highly saturated, and even though it contains no cholesterol, it may be converted into fat products after it is absorbed. Most vegetable oils can be converted from their natural liquid form to a more solid form by hydrogenation, a process that saturates them with hydrogen.

Cholesterol-Lowering Diet

The level of cholesterol and other fats in the blood is influenced by the amount and character of fats we consume in our diet. Diets rich in cholesterol and saturated fats tend to raise the blood cholesterol level, whereas diets rich in polyunsaturated fats and low in saturated fats

NUTRIENT	STEP 1 DIET	STEP 2 DIET
Total Fat	Less than 30% of total calories	Less than 30% of total calories
Saturated Fat	Less than 10% of total calories	Less than 7% of total calories
Polyunsaturated fatty acids	Up to 10% of total calories	Up to 10% of total calories
Monounsaturated fatty acids	10 to 15% of total calories	10 to 15% of total calories
Carbohydrates	50 to 60% of total calories	50 to 60% of total calories
Protein	10 to 20% of total calories	10 to 20% of total calories
Cholesterol	Less than 300 mg per day	Less than 200 mg per day
Total calories	Achieve and maintain desirable weight	Achieve and maintain desirable weight

Figure 22. American Heart Association recommended dietary therapy for hypercholesterolemia.

and cholesterol tend to reduce blood fat levels or to maintain them at low levels.

Foods can be classified into three groups: those that raise the cholesterol level, such as butter, eggs, and cheese; a second group that actually tends to lower cholesterol levels, such as oat bran; and a third group, including carrots, lettuce, fruits, and breads, that has no effect on blood fats. It should be noted, however, that consuming relatively large quantities of dried beans, such as lentils and pinto, navy, red, lima, and northern beans, and eating vegetables such as broccoli and cauliflower, has been reported to lower blood cholesterol levels.

There are many diet plans available for reduction of dietary fats, but none is better than the American Heart Association Step 1 diet (see Figure 22, above). This diet is constructed to accomplish the following goals:

1. Substitute polyunsaturated and monounsaturated fats for saturated fats (which should be less than 10 percent of total calories). Polyunsaturated fats are commonly found in soft margarines, shortening, and vegetable oils such as safflower, sunflower, corn, soybean, and cotton-

seed oils. Margarines vary significantly in their degree of saturation; the more saturated they are, the more solid they are at room temperature. Even though polyunsaturated fats are better than saturated ones, for practical reasons, only small quantities should be used, since a large intake will lead to excess calorie and fat intake, which will make it difficult to achieve the goal outlined in the next paragraph.

2. Reduce total fat intake to no more than 30 percent of the total calories consumed. Currently, approximately 37 to 50 percent of consumed calories in the average American diet is made up of fat products. Foods should be carefully evaluated for total fat content, and obviously those foods with lower fat content should be selected to replace foods with a higher fat content.

3. Reduce dietary cholesterol intake to less than 300 mg per day. As indicated above, cholesterol is found exclusively in animal products, and is not found in foods of vegetable origin. Foods rich in cholesterol include red meats, egg yolks, dairy products, and organ meats such as liver. Some nutritionists claim that eating large amounts of oat bran will increase the amount of cholesterol excreted by the body.

4. Achieve and maintain ideal weight.

5. Be certain that daily requirements for protein, vitamins, minerals, and other nutrients are consumed.

6. Behavior modification can best be achieved if diet changes are made gradually so that they become a natural part of a permanent eating pattern.

7. Develop a "thin mind" through nutritional education and behavior modification.

8. For more details on how best to lower and control your serum cholesterol and other blood lipids, write to obtain one or all of the following educational publications:

- **Promise Margarine "Heart Smart Calculator."** Robert E. Lieberman, Promise Calculator Offer, P. O. Box 973, Medina, Ohio 44258.
- **"So You Have High Blood Cholesterol."** National Cholesterol Educational Program, National Heart, Lung and Blood Institute, Box C-200, NIH, Bethesda, Maryland 20892.
- **"Eating to Lower High Blood Cholesterol."** National Cholesterol Educational Program, National Heart, Lung and Blood Institute, Box C-200, NIH, Bethesda, Maryland 20892.
- **"Coronary Risk Factors: Statement for the American Public."** American Heart Association, National Center, 7320 Greenville Avenue, Dallas, Texas 75231.
- **"Cholesterol and Your Heart."** American Heart Association, National Center, 7320 Greenville Avenue, Dallas, Texas 75231.
- **"The American Heart Association Diet: An Eating Plan for Healthy Americans."** American Heart Association, National Center, 7320 Greenville Avenue, Dallas, Texas 75231.
- **"Recipes for Low-Fat, Low-Cholesterol Meals."** American Heart Association, National Center, 7320 Greenville Avenue, Dallas, Texas 75231.

Summary

The American Heart Association Step 1 Diet Guidelines and the recommendations of the National Heart, Lung and Blood Institute of the National Institutes of Health are as follows:

1. Reduce total fat to less than 30 percent of calories.
2. Reduce saturated fat to less than 10 percent of calories.

3. Reduce cholesterol to less than 100 mg per 1,000 calories consumed, not to exceed 300 mg per day.
4. Reduce sodium to 1 gram per 1,000 calories consumed, not to exceed 3 grams per day.
5. Meet the daily needs for proteins, vitamins, minerals, and other nutrients.
6. Achieve and maintain ideal weight.
7. Substitute poly- and monounsaturated fat for saturated fat whenever possible, but limit polyunsaturated fat to no more than 10 percent of total calories.
8. Obtain 50–60 percent of daily calories from carbohydrates. These changes should be made gradually so that they become a natural part of permanent eating pattern.
9. If serum cholesterol does not diminish at least 10 percent after 8 weeks on the Step 1 Diet, a Step 2 Diet should be undertaken (see Figure 22) in which the cholesterol is reduced to 200 mg per day, the percentage of fat is dropped from 30 percent to 15–20 percent of total calories consumed, and saturated fats constitute no more than 7 percent of the total calories.

If an adequate response in the blood fat pattern does not occur on a Step 2 diet, even more rigid dietary controls, such as the Pritikin regimen, may be used in which cholesterol is reduced to as low as 100 mg per day, with a fat percentage of 10–15 percent of the total calories ingested. If these dietary controls do not prove to be effective, drug therapy (see Chapter 12) should be considered.

Drug therapy should not be employed until a maximum dietary effort has been mounted and sustained. It should be clearly recognized that diet therapy is the mainstay of treatment, regardless of whether or not drugs are used.

How to Stop Smoking

Over 40 million Americans have quit smoking since 1964, and it has been estimated that a similar number would like to quit but have been unable to do so thus far. The obvious solution to this massive health problem is to *prevent* teenagers and young adults from starting to smoke, since this is a much easier task than trying to *stop* smoking once the addiction has been acquired. Antismoking education is more effective if the teenager's parents are nonsmokers; it should be recognized, however, that the major reason for beginning to smoke at a young age is peer pressure. The initial effects of smoking are unpleasant but are easily offset for the teenager by the social "benefits" of smoking, unless these "benefits" have been negated by educational activities in the schools and at home.

Addiction and Behavior

Cigarette smoking has both addicting and behavioral components (see Chapter 5). Nicotine is an addictive drug that, in addition to its chemical actions, has the psychological effect of altering mood and feeling. The Fagerström nicotine tolerance scale questionnaire (see Figure 23) is a nicotine dependency test used to identify the addicted cigarette smoker. The addicted smoker usually smokes within 30 minutes of awakening in the morning, enjoys the first cigarette of the day, smokes more in the morning, smokes even when he or she is ill, inhales the smoke deeply, and will smoke anywhere. The addicted smoker will more likely benefit most from drug treatments such as nicotine gum (see Chapter 12) than will the non-addicted smoker.

Whether or not a smoker is addicted to nicotine, there will almost certainly be a behavioral component to his or her smoking habits. This component of the smoking habit is a "conditioned reflex" similar to that produced in the famous Pavlovian dog, which was trained to salivate every time a bell was sounded because he had been trained to think that he would be fed when the bell rang. Every time a cigarette

	A	B	C
1. How soon after you wake up do you smoke your first cigarette?	After 30 minutes	Within 30 minutes	—
2. Do you find it difficult to refrain from smoking in places where it is forbidden, such as the library, theater, doctor's office?	No	Yes	—
3. Which of all the cigarettes you smoke in a day is the most satisfying one?	Any *other* than the first one in the morning	The first one in the morning	—
4. How many cigarettes a day do you smoke?	1–15	16–26	More than 26
5. Do you smoke more during the morning than during the rest of the day?	No	Yes	—
6. Do you smoke when you are so ill that you are in bed most of the day?	No	Yes	—
7. Does the brand you smoke have a low, medium, or high nicotine content?	Low	Medium	High
8. How often do you inhale the smoke from your cigarette?	Never	Sometimes	Always

Assign no points for each answer in column A, 1 point for each answer in column B, and 2 points for each answer in column C (note that not all questions have an answer in column C). Then total the number of points to arrive at the Fagerström score. The highest possible score is 11.

Those who score 7 or more are highly dependent on nicotine; those who score 6 or less have low to moderate nicotine dependence. Bear in mind that a low score does not rule out the use of nicotine chewing gum or other therapy based on physiologic nicotine addiction. In general, however, the higher the score, the better the result of such therapy.

Figure 23.   The Fagerström nicotine tolerance test.

smoker performs a certain activity—such as drinking a cup of coffee, picking up a telephone, or sitting in a favorite easy chair—he automatically and unconsciously tends to light a cigarette. These behavioral cues are difficult to control unless they are intellectually understood and recognized for what they are; a smoker should therefore carefully complete a daily cigarette diary (see Figure 24) recording his or her pattern of smoking, including the apparent reasons why cigarettes are smoked at a particular moment—pleasure, release of stress, and so on. Completing a cigarette diary will make the smoker aware of when and why each cigarette is smoked, and alternatives to those cigarettes can then be planned.

Motivation and Accomplishment

A carefully structured and intellectual approach is necessary to overcome conditioned reflex patterns. If motivation is adequate and combined with a well-designed self-help program, most smokers can stop "cold turkey" on their own.

The first few days or weeks are the most difficult, because of withdrawal symptoms that occur in smokers who are nicotine-dependent; during this time, interaction with one's physician and support from friends or structured organizations can be of great help. Behavioral changes such as avoiding situations that ordinarily result in lighting up a cigarette (e.g., substituting juices for coffee, leaving matches across the room when one is on the phone), and instituting new positive habits is helpful. Alternatives to cigarettes that will occupy the hands as well as the mouth include handling objects such as a pen, pencil, "worry beads," rubber bands, or paper clips, or sucking on sugarless hard candies, toothpicks, lollipops, swizzle sticks, or chewing gum. The "oral fixation" of many smokers can also be gratified by substitutes which will not result in weight gain, such as carrot sticks, cauliflower sections, celery, and the like. A stringent weight-reduction diet should not be started when one is attempting to stop smoking; however, high-calorie foods should be avoided in

Time of Awakening ————————— Date: —————

Number of cigarettes	Time	Need: 1=least, 10=most	Place and activity	Reason for smoking
— 1				
— 2				
— 3				
— 4				
— 5				
— 6				
— 7				
— 8				
— 9				
—10				
—11				
—12				
—13				
—14				
—15				
—16				
—17				
—18				
—19				
—20				

Figure 24. Daily cigarette diary.

order not to substitute another problem (weight gain) after one has been removed.

The smoker's usual response of lighting a cigarette when under stress or even at times of relaxation should be replaced by other activities such as active social interactions, low-calorie eating, and exercise; in fact, a regular program of exercise will help substitute positive cardiovascular benefits for the undesirable ones produced by nicotine. Motivation can be improved if the person understands that smoking cessation will have both the long-term benefits of avoiding heart attacks, sudden death, lung cancer, chronic bronchitis, emphysema, and other problems, and the short-term improvements in health that occur because of the elimination of such symptoms as lightheadedness, weakness, malaise, agitation, and anxiety. Ex-smokers will feel a sense of accomplishment when the dragon is slain; they will have an improved self-image and sense of well-being, and will take great pride in their ability to conquer this most noxious habit.

A number of self-help programs and kits are listed below that are available to help the motivated person stop smoking. They are free of charge, very educational, and frequently most effective.

- **"I Quit Kit"** may be obtained from the American Cancer Society, 4 West 35th Street, New York, New York 10001, (212) 736-3030, or from your local American Cancer Society Chapter.
- **"A Lifetime of Freedom from Smoking"** and **"Freedom from Smoking in 20 Days"** may be obtained from the American Lung Association, 1740 Broadway, New York, New York 10019, or from your local Lung Association Chapter.
- **"Quit for Good"** kit for physicians, which includes free materials for patients, may be obtained by physicians from the National Cancer Institute, Office of Cancer Communications, Bldg. 31, Room 10A18, Bethesda, Maryland 20892, 1 (800) 422-6237.
- **"Smoking and Heart Disease"** may be obtained from the American Heart Association, National Center, 7320 Greenville Avenue, Dallas, Texas 75231.
- **"Calling It Quits,"** including brochures titled "How to Quit," a guide to help you stop smoking, and "The Good Life," a guide to becoming an ex-smoker, may be obtained from the American Heart Association, National Center, 7320 Greenville Avenue, Dallas, Texas 75231.
- **"Weight Control Guidance in Smoking Cessation"** may be obtained from the American Heart Association, National Center, 7320 Greenville Avenue, Dallas, Texas 75231.

Sedentary Lifestyle

"I never have enough time to exercise, as I did in college." A common complaint in our fast-moving society, yet my closest friend runs a $4-billion-a-year corporation and is on the tennis court every day at 5:00 P.M.; he simply makes it a way of life, and all of his family and business associates have come to accept the fact that that is where he will be at that time. Equally important, after playing tennis he relaxes with his close friends to ease the stress of a busy day. His office schedules business meetings for other times, and he is always available for dinner or social engagements by 7:00 to 7:30 P.M. These are his values, this is his way of life . . . and he continues to be in superb health at age 74.

How Important Is Exercise?

In the past, lack of exercise had not been considered a "major" risk factor, but there is no question that it is important among the "minor" risk factors (see Chapter 5). It is one over which we have total control, and if we correct it, it has significant proven benefits. Although the beneficial effects of exercise have long been controversial, numerous scientific studies over recent years have demonstrated a definite statistical link between a sedentary lifestyle and the onset of symptomatic coronary heart disease, specifically heart attacks and sudden death; therefore, exercise has important benefits in that it can prevent or delay these cardiac events.

The Exercise Program

When relatively sedentary persons start to exercise, even by climbing stairs or walking rapidly, their lack of conditioning becomes quickly obvious. They become short of breath, fatigued, and feel a sense of rapid palpitations as their heart pumps at a quicker pace. If the physical activity is repeated day after day with increasing intensity and/or duration, these sensations are soon no longer noted because a "training effect" is achieved; the heart rate increases only slightly, breathing is easier, and fatigue is not apparent. Any thoughtful exercise program should therefore start at a relatively low level of intensity and gradually progress in a carefully prescribed fashion.

Before Exercising

Younger persons can usually exercise without fear of harming themselves; however, even healthy people who are over the age of 30 or who have abnormal cardiovascular risk factors at any age should receive a medical checkup before starting a strenuous exercise program. Also, anyone with a previously abnormal physical examination or electrocardiogram, or a history of heart disease, diabetes, or hypertension should be thoroughly examined medically prior to starting *any* exercise program.

The medical checkup prior to an exercise program should be similar to the examination recommended in Chapter 10. The physician should obtain a history, perform a careful physical examination, obtain the necessary laboratory studies, and, in almost all circumstances, conduct a treadmill stress test prior to instituting the exercise program. This exercise "road test" will determine whether exercise can be performed safely.

Types of Exercise

There are two basic types of exercise, *aerobic* and *anaerobic*. Aerobic exercises are those in which the muscles' demand for oxygen is increased, while anaerobic exercises are those performed without an increase in oxygen demand (see Figure 25). The additional oxygen required by the exercising muscles is brought to them by the increased output of blood from the heart; the amount of blood that is pumped from the heart climbs from a resting volume of 5 liters per minute to over 20 liters per minute, and most of this increase goes to the exercising muscles. In fact, aerobic exercises send so much additional blood to the exercising muscles that the flow through non-exercising tissues, such as the liver, intestines, and kidneys, is reduced. The amount of air (oxygen) used in aerobic exercises tends to be the same amount that is being used up; therefore, these exercises can usually be performed for a long time, which is why they are called endurance exercises. Anaerobic exercises, such as sprinting, use up more oxygen than is taken in and usually lead to exhaustion within a relatively short time. Cardiovascular fitness is more likely to occur with aerobic or dynamic exercises such as cycling, walking, jogging, and swimming. They result in rhythmic contraction and relaxation of large muscle groups and movement of joints. On the other hand, with anaerobic exercises such as weightlifting and pushups, joints tend to move minimally, a marked increase in tension within muscle fibers themselves is produced, and as the tense muscles squeeze the blood vessels, less blood is permitted to flow through these arteries, frequently causing a marked increase in blood pressure and heart stress. Anaerobic exercises will produce an increase in muscle mass, the type of physical conditioning observed in weightlifters; however, heart and lung conditioning of any significant degree will not result. In other words, aerobic exercises condition the heart and blood vessels, whereas anaerobic exercises do not; in fact, anaerobic exercises are more likely to cause angina or even precipitate a heart attack in patients with coronary artery heart disease.

The Exercise Prescription

A properly designed physical training program increases oxygen intake and is designed to tax the heart and lungs. Since it is obviously impossible to measure oxygen intake at home, in the gym, or on the tennis court, we have learned to use the heart rate as a simple objective method for indirectly measuring oxygen uptake. The *maximal heart rate* is the highest level that an individual's heart rate should reach, based upon his or her age and the usual maximum oxygen uptake observed in other individuals of the same age measured at the same time. The relationship of heart rate to oxygen uptake

Best: Aerobic Exercise	**Not So Good:** Anaerobic Exercise
Walking	Sprinting
Running	Weightlifting
Swimming	Water skiing
Cycling	Pushing against wall
Cross-country skiing	Bowling
Jogging	Golf
Lawn mowing	Downhill skiing
Dancing	Doubles tennis
Singles tennis	Baseball
Racquetball	Volleyball
Rope skipping	
Calisthenics	

Figure 25.   Types of exercise.

remains relatively consistent for persons of all ages and at all levels of training under the usual training circumstances; the correlation is significant enough to permit us to use the maximal heart rate as the prime method for determining the ideal exercise level for any individual.

The effects of exercise are most beneficial when what is known as the *target heart rate* is achieved for a period of 20 to 30 minutes, three or four times per week. One's target heart rate can be calculated by first determining the predicted maximal heart rate and then calculating the target heart rate from that figure. The predicted maximal heart rate for physically inactive and unconditioned individuals is the number 220 minus one's age, whereas, for well-conditioned patients, it is 205 minus one-half the age. The target heart rate zone is 70 to 85 percent of the predicted maximal heart rate, since anything above 85 percent has little benefit (and is potentially dangerous) and anything below 60 to 70 percent is probably not adequate to achieve cardiovascular fitness, although some studies have demonstrated improvement even if only 45 percent is achieved.

For example, a physically inactive man of 40 years of age would have a predicted maximal heart rate of 220 minus 40, or 180 beats per minute. His target heart rate would therefore be 70 to 85 percent of 180, or 128 to 153 beats per minute. If the same individual were conditioned, his predicted maximal heart rate would be 205 minus one-half of 40, or 185. The target heart rate in this instance would then be 130 to 157 beats per minute.

Exercise Frequency, Intensity, and Duration

The easiest way to count the pulse is to count it at the wrist, just below the base of the thumb, or over the carotid artery in the neck (located on either side of the Adam's apple); the pulse should be counted for ten seconds and then multiplied by six, giving the pulse rate per minute.

Initially, the intensity of the exercise program should be sufficient to raise the heart rate to 60 percent of the calculated maximal heart rate; exercise intensity should then be gradually increased weekly until the heart rate climbs to between 70 and 85 percent of the calculated maximal heart rate. The exercise duration should be only five to ten minutes initially, and then should be gradually extended until the target heart rate can be sustained for 20 to 30 minutes in each of the sessions. During these early phases, exercise can be alternated between low-intensity activities, such as walking or slow jogging, and high-intensity ones, such as vigorous swimming or running.

For most people, exercising aerobically for 20 to 30 minutes four times per week (although a daily program is certainly not harmful) and getting the heart rate up in the range of 120 and 140 beats per minute will almost certainly be sufficient to improve cardiovascular fitness. In well-conditioned persons, the rate should return to the resting level within two minutes after cessation of exercise. As physical conditioning improves, the intensity and duration of the exercise program will have to be increased in order to maintain the training effect, since, after several months of exercise, the same amount of swimming or jogging will not increase the heart rate to the degree that it did at the beginning of the training program.

Warm-Up and Cool-Down

A warm-up phase should precede any period of vigorous exercise in order to stretch and loosen up ligaments and muscles, thereby reducing the risk of joint or muscle injury. The warm-up should last at least three to five minutes and should include such exercises as slow toe touching, bending the torso from side to side with the arms extended over the head, or any other exercise that stretches the leg and back muscles and extends the spine. Calisthenics or weight training should not be performed prior to aerobic exercise, but rather should be deferred until the end of the dynamic aerobic workout. A cool-down period of at least five minutes after completing the exercise is also recommended. During exercise, the blood vessels in the body and especially in the arms and legs become dilated; this may result in a diminished flow of blood back to the heart, with associated sensations of dizziness or even fainting. A cool-down period permits the dilated blood vessels to constrict back down to normal size and the heart rate to slow; therefore it is wise to continue walking and moving about for the five minute post-exercise period. Going immediately into a sauna, steam room, or whirlpool, or even sitting down to rest, may lead to lightheadedness or fainting.

Types of Exercise

A specific exercise program should consider a variety of factors including individual physical capability and overall health, the weather and seasonal variations, and, *most important*, the individual's particular exercise preferences, taking into account facilities and equipment required, and their time schedule or availability.

The dynamic aerobic activity chosen should provide enough exercise to produce cardiovascular fitness and be pleasurable and non-competitive, and should be able to fulfill the following requirements:

- A warm-up period of five to ten minutes.
- Endurance training of 30 minutes.

- A five-minute cool-down period (although this may be extended to 20 or 30 minutes by recreational activities).
- If desired, some time should be allotted for structured weight training, since some exercise physiologists feel that weight training after an aerobic program improves compliance and contributes to endurance.

Although over 30 types of exercise qualify as aerobic, the top six are walking, swimming, cycling, cross-country skiing, and jogging or running (see Figure 25). Walking is the most convenient, safest, and effective exercise for patients over the age of 50 with or without known heart disease. You should start such an exercise program by walking two miles in a one-hour period; each week reduce the time by five minutes such that in the second week the two miles are walked in 55 minutes, the third week in 50 minutes, and so on. After achieving a rate that permits you to walk two miles in 30 minutes, the length of the walk can be extended to three miles in 45 minutes. This is an excellent, safe exercise program that is best for relatively in-active patients, whether or not they have known heart disease.

Swimming is a total-body-conditioning exercise, which, because of the buoyancy of water, protects participants from significant tendon, muscle, or bone problems. It is especially good for patients who may have arthritic or musculoskeletal problems. Swimming is best if done three or four times weekly. The time should be gradually increased from 12 minutes to 30 minutes, and the distance in each session from 200 to 900 yards; by the end of the tenth or twelfth week, cardiovascular fitness will be achieved. Simple paddling or floating around in the water has absolutely no positive effect on cardiovascular fitness.

Cycling is an effective aerobic exercise whether done outdoors on a regular bicycle or indoors on a stationary one. It is appealing to many because of the joy of changing terrain and conditions when outdoors; indoors, many people enjoy reading or watching television while exercising. Computerized cycles have made stationary cycling quite interesting, since various types of terrain and difficulties can be simulated, and both heart action and caloric expenditures can be carefully monitored. Virtually all indoor cycle manufacturers supply programs that are acceptable from a cardiovascular fitness point of view, since the resistance of a stationary cycle's wheel can be regulated to achieve the desired goals.

Aerobic exercise workouts, whether done individually or in classes, are being employed with increasing frequency by many individuals. Combining exercise with music is enjoyable, but of course the exercise should be performed at an intensity level sufficient to achieve the target heart rate for at least 20 to 30 minutes. As with all forms of exercise, warm-up and cool-down periods are absolutely essential.

Is Exercise Safe?

Obviously, injuries can occur as a result of exercise, especially to the musculoskeletal system of the lower extremities. Extremes of temperature may lead to heat exhaustion and, in colder climates, to frostbite. A variety of other minor abnormalities, including blood in the urine, diarrhea, and gastrointestinal bleeding, may occur; however, these are extremely rare problems.

The major serious potential complications to be concerned with are heart attacks or sudden death. The risk of an exertion-related heart attack or heart arrest is extraordinarily low if the treadmill test is normal and if target heart rates are not exceeded. Major cardiovascular problems resulting from exercise training are extremely rare, and when they occur, it is usually in persons who have not been adequately pretested for silent heart disease. In all respects, carefully planned and supervised exercise appears to be extremely safe.

12

How to Prevent Heart Attacks and Sudden Death: What Your Doctor Should Be Doing for You

Those who develop heart symptoms have first gone through a pre-symptom phase in which the heart disease is latent (i.e., silent or smoldering), during which time it is almost certainly detectable by the testing procedures outlined in Chapter 10. In this phase we can usually still delay, halt, or even cause a regression of the developing coronary artery problem. What should a doctor do in order to prevent progression and complications of coronary heart disease, and if correctable problems are present, what treatments should be started?

Uncontrollable Risk Factors

Neither the patient nor the physician can change uncontrollable risk factors; however, if any or all of these factors, such as advanced age, male sex, and positive family history (see Chapter 5), are present, the doctor should become more active and aggressive in his recom-mendations and treatment of any of the *controllable* risk factors (see below) that are abnormal, since these patients are at higher risk of developing coronary heart problems. In other words, although treat-able abnormal risk factors should always be corrected, it is especially important to correct them in patients who are older, who have significant family histories of premature heart disease, and/or who are men. Uncontrollable risk factors therefore need to be taken into account only in terms of determining the degree of vigor the physician applies toward controlling the treatable risk factors and to help determine which drug therapy should best be employed in connection with changes in lifestyle and habit patterns.

Controllable Major Risk Factors

High Blood Cholesterol

It has been emphasized previously (see Chapter 11) that instituting an appropriate diet is the *first* approach in the treatment of abnormal blood fats, including elevated cholesterol. A low-fat, low-cholesterol diet that is low in saturated fats and, if necessary, is calorie-controlled, should be all that is needed for most people to achieve a meaningful reduction in abnormally elevated blood cholesterol levels. The physician should guide, support, provide necessary information, and even, in some instances, arrange for professional nutritional counseling. However, if dietary intervention does not achieve normal levels of blood cholesterol, LDL, HDL, and triglycerides, drug therapy should be considered.

Cholesterol-lowering drugs act in the two following basic ways: (1) they either prevent the absorption of ingested and body-manufactured cholesterol from the stomach and intestines (see below), or (2) they decrease the amount of cholesterol manufactured in the liver.

Bile Acid Sequestrants

Bile acid sequestrants are drugs that prevent the reabsorption of cholesterol-containing bile acids, and thereby help rid the body of cholesterol by binding it to the stool.

Colestid (colestipol HCl)

This drug comes in a granular form that has to be mixed with water or other liquids before ingesting. Like Questran (see below), it may cause gastrointestinal complaints. It can be taken with cereals, soups, or fruits two to four times daily and is quite effective in lowering the blood cholesterol and LDL levels. It may delay or reduce the absorption of other oral medications, and therefore the interval between the administration of Colestid and any other medication should be as long as possible.

Questran (cholestyramine).

Patients usually take one to six doses of this powder dissolved in water, soup, or pulpy foods. It will lower elevated serum cholesterol and LDL while raising HDL levels. Although somewhat inconvenient to take, it is effective, with only minimal risk of side reactions (e.g., constipation, nausea, vague abdominal distress); because it prevents absorption of fat molecules, it can result in a reduction of the body's ability to absorb fat-soluble vitamins such as Vitamins A, D, and K, but this risk is minimal.

Drugs That Reduce Cholesterol Manufacture in the Liver

Atromid S (clofibrate)

This drug lowers cholesterol levels only slightly, but has a significant impact on lowering blood triglycerides, with improvement in the serum HDL levels. It is usually given in a dosage of two tablets twice daily, and if side effects occur, they are usually minor.

Lopid (gemfibrozil)

This fat-regulating agent primarily lowers serum triglycerides, with a variable reduction in total serum cholesterol levels. It is usually administered in a dosage of two capsules twice daily. Side effects occur only rarely, usually involving the gastrointestinal system. Dosage of anticoagulants, such as Coumadin, may have to be reduced to prevent bleeding complications if Gemfibrozil is being administered simultaneously.

Lorelco (probucol)

This drug is usually administered in a dosage of two tablets twice daily. It has proven effective in lowering serum cholesterol and LDL cholesterol, with minimal effect on the blood triglyceride levels. It does not lower "good" HDL cholesterol. It may have gastrointestinal side effects similar to the other cholesterol-lowering agents.

Mevacor (lovastatin)

This potent, relatively new drug significantly reduces blood cholesterol and LDL levels, and has either no effect or tends to elevate the HDL levels. It is used in a dosage of only one to four tablets per day. The side effects at this time appear to be minimal; on occasion, reversible liver function abnormalities occur; opacities in the lenses of the eyes have been reported rarely, but these have not been demonstrated to lead to cataracts. It acts by blocking an enzyme in the blood that is involved in the manufacture of cholesterol by the liver. A whole series of new drugs that act this way are currently being tested.

Nicobid, Nicolar (niacin or nicotinic acid)

Niacin is one of the B vitamins (Vitamin B_3), and is manufactured by many pharmaceutical firms in both long-acting and short-acting forms. It tends to lower both serum cholesterol and triglyceride levels and to raise HDL levels. Since it produces dilatation (opening) of the blood vessels in the face, fingers, and toes, often resulting in sensations of flushing, it is best to start with low doses (50 to 250 mg) after meals two or three times daily. If no side effects occur, the long-acting form can be given and the dose gradually built up to as much as 3,000 to 6,000 mg per day. Liver function blood tests have to be taken regularly to be certain that the liver is not being affected adversely.

In addition to the above, combinations of drugs are used on occasion. For example, it has been reported that Colestid used with nicotinic acid has been particularly effective in reducing the total cholesterol level as well as raising the HDL level.

How to Use Cholesterol-Lowering Drugs

There are a number of drug treatment programs. One widely used approach is to measure cholesterol and LDL blood levels every eight weeks; patients should be moved from more liberal diets to more rigid ones if these levels remain abnormally elevated. Drug therapy should be considered only if (1) cholesterol and LDL levels remain high despite appropriate dietary treatment, or, (2) if patients are unable to follow rigid dietary controls. If drug treatment is needed, most physicians prescribe niacin and/or bile acid sequestrants (Questran or Colestid) first; if these produce no effect, a third drug (e.g., Lopid, Atromid S, or Lorelco) is added. If this treatment regimen fails, one of the newer agents, such as Mevacor, should be considered. Many doctors are simply using Mevacor as the first drug of choice because it is so effective; however, for the time being, blood liver function tests have to be followed quite regularly.

There are many drug treatment regimens; your doctor should discuss these methods with you and clearly explain why he or she is selecting one over any other (effectiveness, side effects, ease of use, etc.).

Cigarette Smoking

Physicians exert an enormous influence on their patients, and, therefore, in something as important as cessation of cigarette smoking, physicians should work closely with patients who smoke. Approximately 30 to 40 million cigarette-smoking adults in the United States see their physicians on a regular basis, so doctors are in a position to make a major impact in this enormous public-health issue.

Patients who smoke should be identified and treated as if they were afflicted with a medical problem. It is obviously important to know how long and how much the person has smoked, and whether or not he or she has made previous attempts to stop. Besides the history, a full physical examination and tests of pulmonary function (to discover whether or not the lungs have been affected by the smoking habit) should be performed. The doctor should educate the patient as to how cigarette smoking increases cardiovascular risk and affects lung function. The strong message that smoking is harmful to one's health should be imparted, but, equally important, the physician should focus on and treat all risk factors detected, not just cigarette smoking. For example, if a patient has had a heart attack or angina, an intensive discussion regarding smoking risk is obviously indicated. If the patient has obstructive lung disease or vascular disease in the legs, the effects of cigarette smoking on these conditions should be emphasized.

Furthermore, patients should be informed regarding both the addictive and behavioral effects of cigarette smoking (see Chapter 11). The doctor should educate the patient on the need for a cigarette diary (see Figure 24) and why the Fagerström nicotine tolerance scale questionnaire (see Figure 23) should be completed. The various alternatives to cigarette smoking, the availability of self-help programs (see Chapter 11), and the possible need for psychiatric therapy or active social counseling should be discussed with the patient. The doctor should strongly emphasize that persons are able to quit smoking if they truly want to, since help is now available in the form of effective behavioral psychotherapy and superb drug treatment.

After assessing the patient's motivation to quit smoking and the level of nicotine dependence, the physician should create a smoking-cessation plan for the motivated patient. The doctor should help the patient set up a quit date, add support by having the smoker return frequently, and, if the patient is motivated yet nicotine-dependent, should prescribe nicotine gum therapy.

Drug Treatment

Nicotine dependence (symptoms of withdrawal when smoking is stopped) is a major reason why people find it hard to stop smoking. A simple drug substitute for the effects of nicotine has been sought for many years, but only recently has an effective drug become available.

Nicotine polacrilex gum (Nicorette) is the first agent that has been demonstrated to improve the quitting rates in smokers because of its effectiveness in diminishing or eliminating many of the withdrawal symptoms. This gum acts by releasing a form of nicotine that is absorbed through the tissues of the oral cavity when it is chewed. It works by maintaining a constant low level of nicotine in the blood, thereby avoiding the peaks and valleys of the nicotine "hit" (the effect that occurs because nicotine is rapidly absorbed through the lungs and goes directly into the bloodstream) caused by cigarette smoking.

Because the nicotine blood level achieved with nicotine gum is in the range of a ten-cigarette-a-day smoker, it makes sense for the heavy smoker (40 to 60 cigarettes per day) to attempt to taper down slowly to approximately 10 or 20 cigarettes per day before quitting and starting use of the gum. This tapering action should take several weeks because if an addicted smoker stops smoking suddenly, withdrawal symptoms will almost certainly develop quickly. Since at-

tempts to gradually taper cigarette consumption are frequently unsuccessful, the heavy smoker may have to quit smoking "cold turkey"
and start using Nicorette gum simultaneously.

How to Use Nicotine Gum

The patient should be taught how to use the gum. It should first be
warmed in the mouth for about a minute and then chewed *slowly* 18
to 20 times. Frequently a "peppery" sensation in the mouth will be
noticed; if this occurs, chewing should be temporarily discontinued,
the gum should be "parked" between a cheek and the teeth, several
slow, deep "cigarette breaths" should be taken, and then chewing
should be started once again. The sequence should be repeated over
and over—that is, chew *slowly,* park the gum, breathe, wait, chew,
park the gum, etc.—for approximately 30 minutes. The patient
should attempt not to swallow excess saliva (it should be ex-
pectorated), since it may produce nausea, hiccups, or vomiting. It is
best not to use the gum immediately following ingestion of acid-
producing foods or drinks (cola, coffee, or tea). A smoker under
treatment should carry the gum with him at all times and should use 7
to 15 pieces per day; he should start chewing *before* he starts to
develop sensations of nicotine withdrawal—that is, before he starts to
feel that he needs a cigarette.

During the first week, one piece of gum should be used for every
cigarette previously smoked. Depending on one's need, the time
between each piece of gum used and the rate of chewing can be
gradually adjusted. Most people find that 10 to 12 pieces of gum are
enough to control their urge to smoke. No more than 30 pieces of
gum should ever be chewed in any one day. After the first week, one
piece of gum is usually needed for every two cigarettes previously
smoked. The nicotine gum should be used for *at least* three months,
but not for more than six months. After three months the use of the
gum should be diminished, initially by skipping every third or fourth
dose or by using only a half-piece of gum on each occasion. The
smoker should follow all of the recommendations suggested in Chap-

11 regarding self-treatment of other risk factors during the time that he or she is using the gum.

Clonidine (clonidine HCl) is a drug whose primary use in the United States has been for the treatment of high blood pressure. Several investigators have found it to be useful in diminishing nicotine or other drug withdrawal symptoms. It is not as effective as nicotine gum; however, clinical trials are now being performed using both an oral form and a skin patch (from which the Clonidine is absorbed through the skin into the bloodstream).

A variety of other drugs have been used, but their results have not been nearly as effective as nicotine gum.

High Blood Pressure

Patients afflicted with *fixed* high blood pressure should be treated to reduce the frequency of heart, brain, and kidney complications. Initially, non-drug treatment approaches should be used; these include weight loss in overweight individuals, a carefully conceived exercise program, reduction of stressful activities with relaxation techniques such as biofeedback (or even meditation), and finally, of course, patients should be advised strongly to discontinue cigarette smoking. Salt intake should be vigorously restricted; foods such as salted peanuts, potato chips, pickles, sauerkraut, and prepared meats should be avoided, but also the salt shaker should never be on the table, package labels should be carefully examined (to eliminate foods containing large amounts of salt), and, if necessary, a dietitian should be consulted.

Drug Therapy for Hypertension

Well over 100 individual drugs or drug combinations are available for the treatment of fixed or sustained elevations of blood pressure. These fall into three major classifications: (1) diuretics, (2) drugs that act upon nerve receptors, and (3) vasodilators.

Diuretics

This class of drugs lowers the blood pressure by increasing elimination of sodium and water in the urine and thereby decreasing total body fluids. In the past, diuretics were the first drugs used for the treatment of high blood pressure; in recent years, however, other classes of drugs have come into increasing use. Diuretics may be used in combination with other drugs, and since they frequently cause large quantities of potassium to be excreted in the urine, supplemental potassium preparations have to be given with most diuretics to avoid symptoms or complications of low potassium levels in the bloodstream; "potassium-sparing" diuretics such as Dyrenium, Diazide, and Maxzide do not require supplemental potassium. Commonly prescribed diuretics include the following:

- Dyrenium (triamterene)
- Hydrodiuril (hydrochlthiozide)
- Lasix (furosemide)
- Zaroxolyn (metolazone)

Drugs that Act upon Nerve Receptors

A variety of drugs act upon nerve receptors centrally (in the brain or spinal column) or peripherally (in other areas of the body, such as the arms or legs).

Beta-blockers are a special category of these widely used drugs that are particularly useful in the treatment of high blood pressure; they are frequently effective using only one dose per day, and on occasion they have to be discontinued if patients develop one of the infrequent complications, such as congestive heart failure, asthma, slow heart rates, fatigue, or a dramatic drop in blood pressure. Beta-blocking agents include the following:

- Blocadren (timolol maleate)
- Corgard (nadolal)
- Inderal (propranolol HCl)
- Lopressor (metoprolol tartrate)
- Normodyne (labetalol HCl)
- Sectral (acebutolol HCl)
- Tenormin (atenolol)
- Trandate (labetalol HCl)
- Visken (pindolal)

Vasodilators

These are drugs that cause vasodilatation or opening of the peripheral blood vessels, and they have been found to be very effective in controlling blood pressure. Initially, the vasodilators used were Aspresoline (hydralazine HCl) and Minoxidil but in recent years a newer class of these drugs, called *calcium channel blockers*, have been found to be particularly effective not only in treating high blood pressure but also in treating problems associated with ischemic heart disease. Calcium channel blockers include the following:

- Adalat (nifedipine)
- Calan (verapamil HCl)
- Cardene (nicardine HCl)
- Cardizem (diltiazem HCl)
- Isoptin (verapamil HCl)
- Procardia (nifedipine)

A second new class of these drugs are *angiotensin (or ACE) inhibitors*. They lower blood pressure by altering a biological control mechanism, the *renin-angiotensin system*. Renin is a hormone-like material produced by the kidneys that stimulates the production of angiotensin, a substance that tends to elevate the blood pressure. ACE inhibitors lower the blood pressure by blocking the actions of angiotensin. ACE inhibitors are now frequently used for the treatment of other cardiac problems such as congestive heart failure. They include:

- Capoten (captopril)
- Vasotec (enalapril maleate)

How to Treat Hypertension

Once a physician has decided that drug treatment for hypertension is necessary, he should follow the patient carefully, since a second drug frequently has to be added if blood pressure is not controlled by the drug initially chosen. Combinations of drugs (diuretics with beta-blockers, diuretics with calcium channel blockers, etc.) are frequently prescribed in a single-tablet form; however, the initial control of blood pressure is best achieved by prescribing ingredients separately in order to be certain that the desired effects are achieved and that no complications or problems arise.

Once control of the blood pressure has been normalized, patients should not stop the medications unless directed to do so by their physician, because recurrence of the high blood pressure again puts the patient at risk for developing complications (i.e., heart attacks, strokes, kidney disorders, etc.).

Controllable Minor Risk Factors

Sedentary Lifestyle

Most people have no problem in participating in a sensible exercise program if the necessary motivation and determination are present. Before starting a strenuous exercise program, a complete medical checkup is indicated for everyone over the age of 40 (since at least 10 percent of apparently normal individuals in this age group have disorders of the bones or muscles, or hidden heart disease), and in everyone of any age who has abnormal cardiovascular risk factors or a history of heart disease.

Besides the usual history, physical examination, and biochemical and X-ray studies, a treadmill stress test is necessary to determine what degree of exercise the individual can perform safely. The doctor, after careful study of the results of these evaluations, should formulate an "exercise prescription," which, simply stated, indicates to the patient which aerobic exercise or groups of exercises he or she should perform to achieve maximal benefit. More important, the exercise prescription will guide the patient as to *which exercises can be performed safely*, with minimal or no risk of cardiovascular complications.

A simple exercise prescription for a healthy adult could be as follows:

Frequency:	3–5 times a week
Intensity:	Greater than, or equal to, 70 percent of the maximal heart rate
Duration:	20–60 minutes of continuous activity, depending on intensity
Type:	Aerobic (see Chapter 11)

Obesity

It has been clearly demonstrated that weight reduction may be life-saving for patients with morbid or extreme obesity, defined as 100 pounds overweight or twice one's desirable weight. In this context, desirable weight is the midpoint of the range for a medium-built individual in the Metropolitan Life Insurance Company table (Figure 20), but newer tables also take into account one's age, which may be more specific than sex or body build (Figure 21). Weight reduction should definitely be recommended to persons whose excess body weight is even only 10 to 20 percent above the desirable weight, but is also indicated even in persons with lesser degrees of obesity, especially if they have positive risk factors such as diabetes or hypertension.

The role of the doctor is pivotal in achieving weight loss in over-weight patients. Individual dietary prescriptions formulated by a well-trained nutritionist working with the doctor are effective, but it is the doctor who must be the one to encourage, cajole, reassure, and motivate. The patient who lacks motivation will not even consult his doctor; therefore, by the time a patient consults his physician, he is already a motivated candidate for weight control.

In addition to the nutritional approach to obesity discussed in Chapter 11, the physician has available to him a variety of other methods, both surgical and nonsurgical, for treating morbid obesity. If any of these are used, however, they must be combined with an appropriate dietary regimen and nutritional counseling, since it has been clearly demonstrated that drug and/or surgical techniques used alone do not result in lasting control of the obesity problem.

Drugs for Treatment of Obesity

Appetite-suppressant drugs are of two varieties, amphetamines and non-amphetamines.

Amphetamines stimulate the central nervous system, thereby elevating the blood pressure; in some individuals they are effective in appetite suppression. These drugs have a high potential for abuse and should be used only when alternative weight-reduction therapy has been totally ineffective—in other words, only as a last resort. They should be used only rarely, under careful medical supervision, and for only limited, relatively short periods of time. Government regula-tory agencies control these drugs as they do narcotics, and require special prescriptions before the pharmacist can dispense them. Amphetamines used most commonly include:

- Desoxyn (methamphetamine HCl)
- Dexedrine (dextroamphetamine sulfate)
- Didrex (benzphetamine HCl)

Well over twenty varieties of non-amphetamine drugs are available as adjunctive treatment in weight-reduction regimens. Most of these have drug activity similar to the amphetamines. They usually produce some degree of central nervous stimulation and, at the same time, *in some cases,* reduce appetite. Since it is easy to become dependent on these drugs and since tolerance to the effects of appetite-suppressant drugs may develop within weeks, even non-amphetamine drugs should be administered under careful medical supervision and should be discontinued if drug dependence or other complications occur. The following is a list of some non-amphetamine drugs:

- Bontril (phendimetrazine tartrate)
- Dexatrim (phenylpropanolamine)
- Fastin (phentermine HCl)
- Ionamin (phentermine resin)
- Pondimin (fenfluramine HCl)
- Preludin (phenmetrazine HCl)
- Sanorex (mazindol)
- Tenuate (diethylpropion HCl)
- Tepanil (diethylpropion HCl)

Food Additives

Food additives have been used for many years to suppress appetite. One of the oldest agents in this category is *guar gum.* Guar gum powder, when dissolved in water, turns into a gel-like mass in the stomach and reduces appetite by providing a sense of "fullness." The mass usually dissipates in three or four hours. Results of obesity treatment with additives such as guar gum are not consistent. It should be noted that guar gum treatment has been demonstrated to lower blood cholesterol levels effectively in some individuals.

Surgical Techniques

Surgical procedures have been used to treat morbidly obese individuals on occasion. These include decreasing the size of the stomach surgically (gastric stapling) and surgical diversion techniques, whereby the food contents in the stomach and intestines are diverted, thus decreasing absorption of food products. Surgery still is being recommended for carefully selected individuals; since complications can and do occur, however, it is obviously important to reserve these techniques for patients whose obesity is severe enough to threaten life and who have not responded to more conservative techniques of diet control.

Mechanical Methods

A series of mechanical methods have been used in the past to reduce appetite. One recent method was the insertion of a vinyl balloon into the stomach via a gastroscope (a lighted stomach tube). The balloon was left in place for three months, and weight loss ensued in some individuals, apparently owing to appetite suppression. The balloon technique is no longer being used because of the risk of complications.

Diabetes

Diabetes is one of the leading public health problems in the world, since it affects nearly 10 million people.

It is readily diagnosable and treatable. The physician's approach to control should be (1) weight reduction to ideal levels and (2) control of blood sugar, either by diet or, if necessary, by insulin or one of the many available other drugs. Blood fat levels frequently improve as fasting blood sugars are brought from elevated to normal levels.

While it is beyond the scope of this book to discuss the physician's entire involvement in the control and treatment of diabetes, it is obviously important to recognize that patients with diabetes must always be under careful medical supervision for both diet and drug control.

Antidiabetic Agents

By injection:

- Insulin
  A variety of rapid-acting, intermediate-duration, and long-lasting insulins are available.

Orally:

- Diabeta (glyburide)
- Diabinese (chlorpropamide)
- Dymelor (acetohexamide)
- Glucotrol (glipizide)
- Micronase (glyburide)
- Orinase (tolbutamide)
- Tolinase (tolazamide)

Stress and Personality Type

The effects of stress and personality type on heart disease and its treatment have been discussed extensively in Chapter 6. If adequate support and encouragement cannot be provided by the physician, referral to a psychiatrist or psychologist should be considered. The elimination or reduction of anxiety-provoking stresses appears to help in the prevention and treatment of coronary heart disease problems.

Cardiac rehabilitation programs (used primarily after acute heart attacks or heart surgery) provide great psychological support and contribute to improvement of the patient's cardiovascular condition. Skilled professionals, including physicians, psychologists, nurses, dietitians, social workers, and physical therapists, can all help the patient to reduce his or her degree of stress. Stress diminishes as both patients and their families are educated in the recognition, prevention, and treatment of heart problems.

More than 50 different varieties of antidepressant and tranquilizing drugs are available for patient support if needed. Since these tend to be habit-forming, they should be used carefully, under physician supervision. Long-term use of any agent in the treatment of stress should be avoided. Antidepressants are spectacular drugs for the treatment of some forms of aggressive-depressive behavior, but they are difficult to use properly, and are best used only by physicians skilled in this area. Tranquilizers tend to be addictive and should be used sparingly for the treatment of stressful reactions, and not for long periods. Some of the more widely used antidepressant drugs are:

- Amitriptyline HCl
- Desyrel (trazodone HCl)
- Norpramin (desipramine HCl)
- Pamelor (nortriptyline HCl)
- Pertofrane (desipramine HCl)
- Tofranil (imipramine HCl)
- Triavil (perphenazine and amitriptyline HCl)

The following is a list of some commonly prescribed tranquilizers:

- Ativan (lorazepam)
- Diazepam
- Mellaril (thioridazine)
- Miltown (meprobamate)
- Thorazine (chlorpromazine)
- Tranxene (clorazepate dipotassium)
- Valium (diazepam)
- Xanax (alprazolam)

C H A P T E R

13

Drug Treatment of Silent or Painful Myocardial Ischemia

As I have repeatedly stressed in previous chapters, chest pain is an inaccurate indicator of the degree of poor coronary artery blood flow, since, at most, only 25 percent of all ischemic episodes are painful. As a result, an increasing number of cardiologists have become dissatisfied with the concept that *only* chest pain should be treated in the usual heart patient. Since *silent* episodes of ischemia are totally unknown to the patient, and since what is called the *total ischemic burden* (the frequency, severity, and degree of inadequate coronary artery blood flow, painful or symptom-free) relates significantly to outlook and complications of heart disease, such as heart attack or sudden death, the prognosis for patients with coronary heart disease involves much more than simply whether or not chest pain is present and/or treated.

Modification and treatment of abnormal risk factors will effectively improve the ischemic burden, and there is a growing body of evidence to suggest that appropriate drug therapy will have a similar if not a greater impact on reducing the incidence of sudden death and heart attacks. Hundreds of drugs currently are in use for the treatment of heart patients; however, with respect specifically to angina and silent ischemia, the drugs used fall into three main categories: (1) nitrates, (2) beta-blockers, and (3) calcium channel blockers.

Nitrates

Nitrates have been used in one form or another since 1867, and are still the most common medications that physicians use to treat patients with angina pectoris. They act by relaxing the muscular walls of both arteries and veins, thereby (1) opening up the coronary arteries, permitting more oxygen-rich blood to flow to the heart muscle itself, and (2) dilating arteries and veins in the periphery (the arms and legs), diminishing the amount of work done by the heart, and reducing its oxygen requirements. They are administered either under the tongue or orally (tablets and capsules), in both regular and long-acting forms.

Nitroglycerine is a rapidly acting nitrate that is administered under the tongue and is the treatment of choice for acute anginal chest pains; it may also be administered as an ointment or via convenient drug patches applied to the skin.

Nitrates reduce both symptomatic and symptom-free episodes of inadequate coronary artery blood flow. In fact, one study reported that intravenous nitroglycerine infusions eliminated *all* episodes of silent ischemia. Common examples of nitrates are:

- Cardilate (erythrityl tetranitrate)
- Dilatrate (isosorbide dinitrate)
- Isordil (isosorbide dinitrate)
- Nitro-Bid (nitroglycerine)
- Nitrodisc (nitroglycerine)
- Nitro-Dur (nitroglycerine)
- Nitrol Ointment (nitroglycerine)
- Nitrospan (nitroglycerine)
- Nitrostat (nitroglycerine)
- Sorbitrate (isosorbide dinitrate)
- Transderm-Nitro (nitroglycerine)

Beta-Blockers

As noted previously, beta-blockers are drugs that block certain nerve endings in the heart. They are extremely effective in the treatment of high blood pressure and tend to slow the heartbeat as well as to diminish the force of the heart's contractions and the amount of oxygen needed. Beta-blockers reduce the amount of work performed by the heart, and have been demonstrated to significantly decrease the number of ischemic episodes, both painful and silent. For a list of beta-blocking agents, see page 149.

Calcium Channel Blockers

Calcium antagonists, called calcium channel blockers, block the entry of calcium into the muscle cells of the heart and blood vessels. As mentioned earlier, they belong to a class of drugs known as vasodilators (drugs that open up the artery channels) and have proven to be extremely effective in the treatment of angina, hypertension, and some malfunctions of heart rhythm.

Calcium channel blockers appear to significantly decrease the total ischemic burden and reduce the incidence of episodes of silent myocardial ischemia. When beta-blockers are added to calcium channel blockers, the degree of improvement frequently is greater than when either agent is used alone. For a list of calcium channel blockers, see page 149.

Other Drugs

Mexitil (mexiletine HCl) therapy has been demonstrated to produce a significant decrease in the number of painful episodes of ischemia, but did not result in a significant decrease in the number of silent episodes. Intravenous aspirin used on one study did not decrease the number of ischemic episodes; however, many scientific studies have shown that antiplatelet drugs (aspirin or Persantine) may reduce the risk of recurrent heart attacks, strokes, the complications of unstable angina, and the frequency of graft closure (i.e., after coronary artery bypass surgery). Its effectiveness in the treatment of ischemia, painful or not, is uncertain at this time, but most cardiologists are administering aspirin daily or every other day to patients with known or suspected coronary artery disease unless there are specific reasons not to do so. They are also prescribing it as a preventative, that is, to delay or prevent the onset of symptomatic coronary artery disease and/or strokes.

Summary

Available evidence seems to suggest that the goal in treating patients with SMI is the complete eradication of the entire ischemic burden, that is, all ischemic episodes, whether painful or silent. Treadmill stress tests as well as Holter monitoring should be used to follow the results and to determine whether or not drug treatment is effective. The choice of drugs used to treat SMI is not different from the choice of drugs available for the treatment of painful angina.

As of the date of publication of this book, many cardiologists remain uncertain as to how vigorously they should pursue drug treatment of silent ischemic episodes. Extensive epidemiological studies are now in progress that will eventually answer the many questions regarding such treatment; however, until these studies have provided definitive answers, it would seem to make good medical sense to prescribe drug therapy (assuming that there are no adverse effects) to reduce or eliminate *all* of the episodes of SMI, especially in the high-risk person. Of course, coronary artery bypass surgery and/or angioplasty should be considered when indicated, but if medical treatment is selected, drug therapy using one or more of the agents discussed above should be prescribed. Until additional scientific data is available, and unless there are specific contraindications, SMI should be treated as aggressively as painful ischemia.

The anti-ischemic drug or drugs finally selected will depend upon the available medical facts (is the heart rate rapid during the ischemia? does it occur at rest or when exercising? and so on), and is best individualized by the physician after analysis of all of the features in any case. It would appear that beta-blockers and/or calcium channel blockers should be recommended for ischemia of the "demand" type —that is, occurring with exertion or effort—whereas vasodilators (nitrates or calcium channel blockers) should be prescribed for ischemia of the "supply" type, occurring at rest. A recent study published in the famous British medical journal *Lancet* found that a beta-blocker was more effective than a calcium channel blocker used alone; however, combinations of these and other agents in varying dosages will almost certainly prove to be more effective than any drug by itself, because the cause of ischemia in most cases is probably mixed (resulting from both demand and supply factors), and treatment should therefore be individualized.

In any case, we have the drugs. For the time being, and until the unlikely proof is presented that they do not help, *they should be used* in order to prevent SMI, heart attacks, and sudden death. They appear to be lifesaving when used to treat that deadly enemy—silent myocardial ischemia.

[]

Quiz: Risk of Developing Heart Disease

Quiz: Risk of Developing Heart Disease

My age and sex
- 0   woman younger than 50
- +1 woman aged 50–65
- +2 woman older than 65
- +1 man younger than 40
- +2 man aged 40–50
- +3 man aged 50–65
- +4 man older than 65   SCORE _____

Among my parents or siblings, there have been heart problems (i.e., heart attacks, angina, sudden death) before the age of 60
- 0   in no parent or sibling
- +1 in 1 or more parents or siblings
  over the age of 60
- +2 in 1 parent or sibling
  under the age of 60
- +4 in 2 or more parents or siblings
  under the age of 60   SCORE _____

Smoking

0   I have never smoked

Smoked in the past:
+1   quit over 5 years ago
+2   quit 2–5 years ago
+3   quit 1–2 years ago
+6   quit less than 1 year ago

I now smoke
+6   Less than 10 cigarettes a day
+8   10–20 cigarettes a day
+16   20–40 cigarettes a day
+20   over 40 cigarettes a day   SCORE _____

Cholesterol and other fats

My serum cholesterol level is
0   170 or less
+1 170–200
+2 200–240
+4 240–300
+6 over 300   SCORE _____

My LDL is
0   130 or less
+2 130–160
+4 160–190
+6 over 190   SCORE _____

My HDL is
0   over 60
+1 45–60
+2 30–40
+3 25–30
+4 less than 25   SCORE _____

Blood pressure

My blood pressure is

(AGE UNDER 60)
0	below 140/90
+4	above 140/90

(AGE 60 OR OLDER)
0	below 140/90
+1	between 140/90 and 180/96
+4	above 180/96

SCORE _____

Diabetes

My fasting blood sugars have always been
0	normal ˏ
+1	occasionally slightly elevated
+3	diabetes after age of 30
+4	diabetes before age of 30

SCORE _____

Exercise

I exercise aerobically (running, vigorous walking, swimming, cycling, etc.)
0	regularly 3–5 times per week
+2	only on weekends
+4	little or none

SCORE _____

Weight

My weight is
0	ideal
+1	5–10% overweight
+2	10–20% overweight
+3	20–30% overweight
+4	over 30% overweight

SCORE _____

Stress

I feel stressed

    0   rarely or not at all

  +1 occasionally

  +2 frequently

  +4 all the time   SCORE _____

Add all scores and interpret your risk of developing symptomatic coronary artery heart disease (i.e., angina, heart attack, sudden death).

                                TOTAL SCORE _____

Interpretation

  0–14 = low risk

14–24 = moderate risk

24 or more = high risk

ⵊⵊ

Helpful Hints for Diet Control

*1. Eating to Lower Your High Blood
   Cholesterol: Sample Menus
2. A Guide to Choosing Foods
   Low in Saturated Fat and
   Cholesterol
3. Food Group Composition*

To effectively follow a low-saturated-fat, low-cholesterol diet, it is absolutely essential to adhere to the following requirements:

- Reduce red meat. Red meat is the principal source of saturated fat and cholesterol in the American diet. The average 80 pounds of red meat per year consumed by each American almost certainly contributes to raising blood cholesterol and putting on additional weight. Servings of red meat should be restricted to only two or three three-ounce servings per week. The meat consumed should not be processed and should be extremely lean. Portions should be extremely limited.
- Make pot roasts or stews one or two days ahead of time. Chill them and then scrape off the fat that collects on the top. Reheat before serving.
- Broil, bake, roast, or barbecue all meats, fish, and poultry. Pan frying or deep-fat frying should be avoided. Basting with wine, broth, lemon, or tomato juice will prevent drying and give good flavor.

- Substitute low-fat sandwich meats for higher-fat cold cuts; use low-fat hot dogs instead of regular varieties.
- Consume more poultry. Poultry is generally lower in calories and fat than red meat. The skin of the fowl should be removed, since it contains a great deal of fat, and if the poultry can be cooked without the skin, the caloric and fat value is diminished. Turkey, especially the light meat, is lowest in fat, calories, and cholesterol.
- Fish products are also lower in calories than is red meat, and, equally important, fish and fish oils have been found to be beneficial with respect to prevention of heart attacks. One possibly beneficial component of fish oil is an unsaturated fat known as *omega-3*, which is reputed (though not yet proven) to be effective in lowering cholesterol and reducing other lipids in the blood. Shellfish, although slightly high in cholesterol, are extremely low in saturated fat and also high in omega-3 unsaturated oils.
- Consume low-fat dairy products. Obviously the amount of fat in dairy products is extremely variable. For example, cream cheese can have over 90 percent fat, whereas nonfat or low-fat milks may have 2 percent or less. Cheese should be avoided since it is frequently 65 to 75 percent fat and very high in calories per unit weight; even "low fat" cheese is relatively high in fat. Always use skim or low-fat milk.
- Use yogurt as a substitute for cream in salad dressing and dips.
- Substitute sherbet, ice milk, or nonfat frozen yogurt for ice cream.
- Discard egg yolks as much as possible and substitute a teaspoon of polyunsaturated oil for each discarded yolk in cooking recipes. Use as many egg whites as you wish, since they are pure protein. Many restaurants now serve yokeless omelettes.

- Reduce the amount of fats in recipes by 33 to 50 percent. For example, if you use commercial cake mixes, buy those to which you must add the fat or oil, substitute a polyunsaturated oil, and reduce the amount by at least 33 percent (while increasing the water content).
- Reduce intake of baked goods made with coconut oil, palm oil, or shortening, and/or those deep-fried in fats (such as doughnuts).
- Instead of two-crust pies, serve single-crust, open-faced pies.
- Use low-calorie dried milk in coffee. Nondairy creamers are generally high in saturated fats.
- Dessert toppings should be made with nonfat dried milk, yogurt, tofu, or fruit. Use a nonstick pan or a vegetable-oil pan coating instead of butter, margarine, or oil when sautéing or frying foods. Spray popcorn lightly with non-stick vegetable coating and then sprinkle on a seasoning such as chili powder, onion powder, or cinnamon, rather than using oil or fat in the preparation.
- Use low-fat cheese, such as part-skim mozzarella and ricotta, in place of regular varieties.
- Limit consumption of cholesterol-rich foods such as whole milk, ice cream, butter, organ meats (especially liver), sour cream, whole-milk yogurt, and cheeses; finally, no more than three egg yolks should be consumed per week (but, as noted above, there is no limit on egg whites).
- Use herbs or herb-flavored croutons to flavor soups and salads. Make your own stuffings with plain bread crumbs. Foods can be coated with crumbs after dipping in a skim-milk-and-egg-white mixture.
- As suggested by the American Heart Association and the National Institutes of Health, carefully record and tabulate totals of calories, cholesterol, saturated fats, and percent of calories made up of saturated fats consumed each

day. These values may be easily tracked by using the "Promise Heart Smart Calculator." For information on how to obtain one of these simple pocket devices, write to Robert E. Lieberman, Promise Calculator Offer, P. O. Box 973, Medina, Ohio 44258.

- Labels of all products that may contain cholesterol or fat should be carefully read prior to purchase. In the relatively near future, most labels will list the exact content of fats, cholesterol, and carbohydrates, and indicate whether the fats are saturated or unsaturated. Compare commercial items side-by-side as illustrated in the following example:

PER SERVING OF STICK MARGARINE— 1 tablespoon (14 grams)	BUTTER	MARGARINES			
		Promise	*Fleishman's*	*Hollywood*	*Mazola*
CALORIES	108	90	100	100	100
FATS (grams)	12	10	11	11	11
Polyunsaturated	1.0	4	4	5	4
Saturated	8.0	2	2	2	2
CHOLESTEROL (milligrams)	30	0	0	0	0
PROTEIN (grams)	0	0	0	0	0
CARBOHYDRATES (milligrams)	0	0	0	0	0
SODIUM (milligrams)	123	90	95	130	100

• Most companies produce margarines in several forms characterized by their nutritional value (regular, low-calorie), consistency (stick, tub), and sodium content (regular, low). Tub margarines have less saturated fat than do the solid, saturated stick margarines. In the commercially available brand used in this example, note that the extra-light tub form has 60 percent of the fat, 53 percent of the calories, and 50 percent of the saturated fat than the regular stick form. From a nutritional point of view, it makes obvious sense to select extra-light tub margaine over all the other forms of the same brand of margarine—but this can be determined only if the labels of each product of each brand are carefully examined.

PER SERVING 1 tablespoon (14 grams)	BUTTER	PROMISE margarine				
		Stick Regular	Stick Light	Tub	Tub Light	Tub-Extra Light
CALORIES	108	90	70	90	70	50
FATS (grams)	12	10	7	10	7	6
Polyunsaturated	1.0	4	3	5	3	3
Saturated	8.0	2	1	1	1	1
CHOLESTEROL (milligrams)	30	0	0	0	0	0
PROTEIN (grams)	0	0	0	0	0	0
CARBOHYDRATES (milligrams)	0	0	0	0	0	0
SODIUM (milligrams)	123	90	65	90	65	50

PER SERVING 1 tablespoon (14 grams)	FLEISCHMAN'S				
	Stick Regular	Stick Light	Tub	Tub Light	Diet Tub
CALORIES	100	80	100	80	50

PER SERVING 1 tablespoon (14 grams)	WEIGHT WATCHERS	
	Stick Regular	Tub
CALORIES	60	50

PER SERVING 1 tablespoon (14 grams)	MAZOLA	
	Stick Regular	Diet Tub
CALORIES	100	50

PER SERVING 1 tablespoon (14 grams)	PARKAY			
	Stick Regular	Tub	Whipped spread Tub	Squeeze Bottle
CALORIES	100	100	60	100

PER SERVING 1 tablespoon (14 grams)	BLUE BONNET	
	Stick Regular	Spread Tub
CALORIES	100	60

PER SERVING 1 tablespoon (14 grams)	HOTEL BAR	
	Stick Regular	Tub Light
CALORIES	100	70

1. Eating to Lower Your High Blood Cholesterol

Sample Menus

AVERAGE AMERICAN DIET (37% FAT)	A NEW LOW-FAT DIET (30% FAT)	A NEW LOW-FAT DIET (30% FAT)
BREAKFAST 1 fried egg 2 slices white toast w/1 teaspoon butter 1 cup orange juice black coffee or tea	**BREAKFAST** 1 cup corn flakes with blueberries 1 cup 1% milk 1 slice rye toast with 1 teaspoon margarine 1 cup orange juice black coffee or tea	**BREAKFAST** 1 cup shredded wheat with peach slices 1 cup 1% milk 1 slice whole wheat toast with 1 tsp margarine 1 cup pink grapefruit juice black coffee
SNACK 1 doughnut	**SNACK** 1 toasted pumpernickel bagel with 1 tsp margarine	**SNACK** 1 toasted English muffin with 1 tsp margarine
LUNCH 1 grilled cheese (2 oz.) sandwich/white bread 2 oatmeal cookies black coffee or tea	**LUNCH** 1 tuna salad (3 oz.) sandwich whole wheat bread with lettuce/tomato 1 graham cracker tea with lemon	**LUNCH** 3 oz. turkey salad on lettuce with tomato wedges 1 thick slice of French bread 10 animal crackers tea with lemon
SNACK 20 cheese cracker squares	**SNACK** 1 crisp apple	**SNACK** 1 banana
DINNER 3 oz. fried hamburger/ketchup 1 baked potato w/sour cream 3/4 cup steamed broccoli with 1 tsp butter 1 cup whole milk 1 piece frosted marble cake	**DINNER** 3 oz. broiled lean ground beef with ketchup 1 baked potato with low-fat yogurt and chives 3/4 cup steamed broccoli with 1 tsp margarine tossed green salad with 1 tbsp oil and vinegar dressing 1 cup 1% milk 1 small piece homemade gingerbread with maraschino cherry/sprig of mint*	**DINNER** 3 oz. broiled halibut with lemon and herb seasoning 1/2 cup brown rice with mushrooms 1 dinner roll with 1 tsp margarine 3/4 cup carrot strips with 1 tsp margarine spinach salad with 1 tsp oil and vinegar dressing 1 cup 1% milk 1 small piece homemade yellow cake*

NUTRIENT ANALYSIS		NUTRIENT ANALYSIS		NUTRIENT ANALYSIS	
Calories	2,000	Calories	2,000	Calories	2,000
Total fat (% of calories)	37	Total fat (% of calories)	30	Total fat (% of calories)	30
Saturated fat (% of calories)	19	Saturated fat (% of calories)	10	Saturated fat (% of calories)	10
Cholesterol	505 mg	Cholesterol	186 mg	Cholesterol	172 mg

*Homemade desserts should be made with unsaturated fats instead of saturated fats. Two egg whites may be substituted for 1 egg yolk.

From "Eating to Lower Your High Blood Cholesterol," National Heart, Lung and Blood Institute, Bethesda, Maryland.

2. A Guide to Choosing Foods Low in Saturated Fat and Cholesterol

Meat, Poultry, Fish, and Shellfish (no more than 6 ounces a day)

CHOOSE	NOT SO GOOD	AVOID
Lean cuts of meat with fat trimmed:		"Prime" grade, Fatty cuts of meat:
• Beef (round sirloin, chuck, loin)		• beef (corned-beef brisket, regular ground, short ribs)
• Lamb (leg, arm, loin, rib)		• pork (spareribs, blade roll, fresh)
• Pork (tenderloin, leg, shoulder)		Duck
• Veal (all trimmed cuts)		Goose, domestic
Poultry without skin		Organ meats
Fish		Sausage, bacon
Shellfish		Reg. luncheon meats
		Frankfurters
		Caviar, roe

Dairy Products (2 servings a day)

CHOOSE	NOT SO GOOD	AVOID
Skim milk, 1% milk, low-fat buttermilk, low-fat evaporated, or nonfat milk	2% milk Yogurt Part-skim ricotta Part-skim or imitation hard cheeses, part-skim mozzarella	Whole milk (regular, evaporated, con-densed)
Low-fat yogurt	"Light" cream cheese	Cream (half-and-half, most nondairy cream-ers, imitation milk products, whipped cream)
Low-fat soft cheeses (cottage, farmer, or pot cheese)	"Light" sour cream	Custard-style yogurt Whole-milk ricotta Neufchatel Brie
Cheeses labeled no more than 2–6 grams of fat per ounce		Hard cheeses (Swiss, American, cheddar, mozzarella, feta, muenster) Cream cheese Sour cream

Fats and Oils (up to 6 to 8 teaspoons a day)

CHOOSE	NOT SO GOOD	AVOID
Unsaturated vegetable oils (corn, olive, peanut, rapeseed/ canola, safflower, sesame, soybean) Margarine or shortening made from un- saturated fats listed above: liquid, tub, stick, diet	Nuts and seeds Avocados and olives	Butter, coconut oil, palm oil, palm kernel oil, lard, bacon fat Margarine or shortening made from saturated fats listed above

Eggs (no more than 3 egg yolks a week)

CHOOSE	NOT SO GOOD	AVOID
Egg whites Cholesterol-free egg sub- stitutes		Egg yolks

Breads, Cereals, Pasta, Rice, Dried Peas and Beans (6 to 11 servings a day)

CHOOSE	NOT SO GOOD	AVOID
Breads (white, whole- wheat, pumpernickel, rye breads, pita, bagel, English muffin, dinner rolls, sandwich buns, rice cakes) Low-fat crackers (matzo, bread sticks, Rye-Krisp, saltines, zwieback) Hot cereals, most cold dry cereals Pasta (plain noodles, spaghetti, macaroni) Any grain rice Dried peas and beans (split peas, black-eyed peas, chick peas, kidney beans, navy beans, lentils, soybeans, soybean curd [tofu])	Store-bought pancakes, waffles, biscuits, muf- fins, cornbread	Croissant, butter rolls, sweet rolls, Danish pastry, doughnuts Most snack crackers (cheese, butter, those made with saturated oils) Granola-type cereals made with saturated oils Pasta and rice prepared with cream, butter, or cheese sauces; egg noodles

Fruits and Vegetables (2 to 4 servings of fruit and 3 to 5 servings of vegetables a day)

CHOOSE	NOT SO GOOD	AVOID
Fresh, frozen, canned, or dried fruits and vegetables		Vegetables prepared in butter, cream, or sauce

Sweets and Snacks (avoid too many)

CHOOSE	NOT SO GOOD	AVOID
Low-fat frozen desserts (sherbet, sorbet, Italian ices, frozen yogurt, popsicles)	Frozen desserts (ice milk)	High-fat frozen desserts (ice cream, frozen tofu)
Low-fat cakes (angel food cake)	Homemade cakes, cookies, pies using unsaturated oils sparingly	High-fat cakes (most store-bought, pound, frosted cakes)
Low-fat cookies (fig bars, ginger snaps)	Fruit crisps and cobblers	Store-bought pies
Low-fat candy (jelly beans, hard candy)		Most store-bought cookies
Low-fat snacks (plain popcorn, pretzels)		Most candy (chocolate bars)
Nonfat beverages (carbonated drinks, juices, tea, coffee)		High-fat snacks (chips, buttered popcorn)
		High-fat beverages (frappés, floats, milk shakes, and egg nogs)

Label Ingredients

Go easy on products that list any fat or oil first, or that list many fat and oil ingredients. The following lists clue you in to names of unsaturated (go easy on these) and saturated-fat ingredients (decrease).

LOW SATURATED	SATURATED
Carob, cocoa	Cocoa butter
Oil: corn, cottonseed, olive, safflower, sesame, soybean, sunflower	Animal fat: bacon, beef, chicken, ham, lamb, meat, pork, or turkey fats; butter, lard
Nonfat dry milk, nonfat dry milk solids, skim milk	Coconut, coconut oil, palm, or palm kernel oil
	Cream
	Egg and egg-yolk solids
	Hardened fat or oil
	Hydrogenated vegetable oil
	Milk chocolate
	Shortening or vegetable shortening
	Vegetable oil (could be coconut, palm kernel, or palm oil)

Adapted from "Eating to Lower Your High Blood Cholesterol," National Heart, Lung and Blood Institute, Bethesda, Maryland.

3. Food Group Composition

MEATS

Product (3½ ounces cooked)	Saturated Fatty Acids (Grams)	Cholesterol (Milligrams)	Total Fat[1] (Grams)	Calories From Fat[2](%)	Total Calories
Beef					
Kidneys, simmered	1.1	387	3.4	21	144
Liver, braised[3]	1.9	389	4.9	27	161
Round, top round, lean only, broiled	2.2	84	6.2	29	191
Round, eye of round, lean only, roasted	2.5	69	6.5	32	183
Round, tip round, lean only, roasted	2.8	81	7.5	36	190
Round, full cut, lean only, choice, broiled	2.9	82	8.0	37	194
Round, bottom round, lean only, braised	3.4	96	9.7	39	222
Short loin, top loin, lean only, broiled	3.6	76	8.9	40	203
Wedge-bone sirloin, lean only, broiled	3.6	89	8.7	38	208
Short loin, tender- loin, lean only, broiled	3.6	84	9.3	41	204
Chuck, arm pot roast, lean only, braised	3.8	101	10.0	39	231
Short loin, T-bone steak, lean only, choice, broiled	4.2	80	10.4	44	214
Short loin, porter- house steak, lean only, choice, broiled	4.3	80	10.8	45	218

MEATS *(continued)*

Product (3½ ounces cooked)	Saturated Fatty Acids (Grams)	Cholesterol (Milligrams)	Total Fat[1] (Grams)	Calories From Fat[2](%)	Total Calories
Brisket, whole, lean only, braised	4.6	93	12.8	48	241
Rib eye, small end (ribs 10–12), lean only, choice, broiled	4.9	80	11.6	47	225
Rib, whole (ribs 6–12), lean only, roasted	5.8	81	13.8	52	240
Flank, lean only, choice, braised	5.9	71	13.8	51	244
Rib, large end (ribs 6–9), lean only, broiled	6.1	82	14.2	55	233
Chuck, blade roast, lean only, braised	6.2	106	15.3	51	270
Corned beef, cured, brisket, cooked	6.3	98	19.0	68	251
Flank, lean and fat, choice, braised	6.6	72	15.5	54	257
Ground, lean, broiled medium	7.2	87	18.5	61	272
Round, full cut, lean and fat, choice, braised	7.3	84	18.2	60	274
Rib, short ribs, lean only, choice, braised	7.7	93	18.1	55	295
Salami, cured, cooked, smoked, 3–4 slices	9.0	65	20.7	71	262
Short loin, T-bone steak, lean and fat, choice, broiled	10.2	84	24.6	68	324

MEATS (continued)

Product (3½ ounces cooked)	Saturated Fatty Acids (Grams)	Cholesterol (Milligrams)	Total Fat[1] (Grams)	Calories From Fat[2](%)	Total Calories
Chuck, arm pot roast, lean and fat, braised	10.7	99	26.0	67	350
Sausage, cured, cooked, smoked, about 2	11.4	67	26.9	78	312
Bologna, cured, 3–4 slices	12.1	58	28.5	82	312
Frankfurter, cured, about 2	12.0	61	28.5	82	315
Lamb					
Leg, lean only, roasted	3.0	89	8.2	39	191
Loin chop, lean only, broiled	4.1	94	9.4	39	215
Rib, lean only, roasted	5.7	88	12.3	48	232
Arm chop, lean only, braised	6.0	122	14.6	47	279
Rib, lean and fat, roasted	14.2	90	30.6	75	368
Pork					
Cured, ham steak, boneless, extra lean, unheated	1.4	45	4.2	31	122
Liver, braised[3]	1.4	355	4.4	24	165
Kidneys, braised[3]	1.5	480	4.7	28	151
Fresh, loin, tenderloin, lean only, roasted	1.7	93	4.8	26	166
Cured, shoulder, arm picnic, lean only, roasted	2.4	48	7.0	37	170
Cured, ham, boneless, regular, roasted	3.1	59	9.0	46	178

MEATS *(continued)*

Product (3½ ounces cooked)	Saturated Fatty Acids (Grams)	Cholesterol (Milligrams)	Total Fat[1] (Grams)	Calories From Fat[2](%)	Total Calories
Fresh, leg (ham), shank half, lean only, roasted	3.6	92	10.5	44	215
Fresh, leg (ham), rump half, lean only, roasted	3.7	96	10.7	43	221
Fresh, loin, center loin, sirloin, lean only, roasted	4.5	91	13.1	49	240
Fresh, loin, sirloin, lean only, roasted	4.5	90	13.2	50	236
Fresh, loin, center rib, lean only, roasted	4.8	79	13.8	51	245
Fresh, loin, top loin, lean only, roasted	4.8	79	13.8	51	245
Fresh, shoulder, blade, Boston, lean only, roasted	5.8	98	16.8	59	256
Fresh, loin, blade, lean only, roasted	6.6	89	19.3	62	279
Fresh, loin, sirloin, lean and fat, roasted	7.4	91	20.4	63	291
Cured, shoulder, arm picnic, lean and fat, roasted	7.7	58	21.4	69	280
Fresh, loin, center loin, lean and fat, roasted	7.9	91	21.8	64	305
Cured, shoulder, blade roll, lean and fat, roasted	8.4	67	23.5	74	287
Fresh, Italian sausage, cooked	9.0	78	25.7	72	323
Fresh, bratwurst, cooked	9.3	60	25.9	77	301

MEATS *(continued)*

Product (3½ ounces cooked)	Saturated Fatty Acids (Grams)	Cholesterol (Milligrams)	Total Fat[1] (Grams)	Calories From Fat[2](%)	Total Calories
Fresh, chitterlings, cooked	10.1	143	28.8	86	303
Cured, liver sausage, liverwurst	10.6	158	28.5	79	326
Cured, smoked link sausage, grilled	11.3	68	31.8	74	389
Fresh, spareribs, lean and fat, braised	11.8	121	30.3	69	397
Cured, salami, dry or hard	11.9	—	33.7	75	407
Bacon, fried	17.4	85	49.2	78	576
Veal					
Rump, lean only, roasted	—	128	2.2	13	156
Sirloin, lean only, roasted	—	128	3.2	19	153
Arm steak, lean only, cooked	—	90	5.3	24	200
Loin chop, lean only, cooked	—	90	6.7	29	207
Blade, lean only, cooked	—	90	7.8	33	211
Cutlet, medium fat, braised or broiled	4.8	128	11.0	37	271
Foreshank, medium fat, stewed	—	90	10.4	43	216
Plate, medium fat, stewed	—	90	21.2	63	303
Rib, medium fat, roasted	7.1	128	16.9	70	218
Flank, medium fat, stewed	—	90	32.3	75	390

POULTRY

Product (3½ ounces, cooked)	Saturated Fatty Acids (Grams)	Cholesterol (Milligrams)	Total Fat[1] (Grams)	Calories From Fat[2](%)	Total Calories
Turkey, fryer-roasters, light meat without skin, roasted	0.4	86	1.9	8	140
Chicken, roasters, light meat without skin, roasted	1.1	75	4.1	24	153
Turkey, fryer-roasters, light meat with skin, roasted	1.3	95	4.6	25	164
Chicken, broilers or fryers, light meat without skin, roasted	1.3	85	4.5	24	173
Turkey, fryer-roasters, dark meat without skin, roasted	1.4	112	4.3	24	162
Chicken, stewing, light meat without skin, stewed	2.0	70	8.0	34	213
Turkey roll, light and dark	2.0	55	7.0	42	149
Turkey, fryer-roasters, dark meat with skin, roasted	2.1	117	7.1	35	182
Chicken, roasters, dark meat without skin, roasted	2.4	75	8.8	44	178
Chicken, broilers or fryers, dark meat without skin, roasted	2.7	93	9.7	43	205
Chicken, broilers or fryers, light meat with skin, roasted	3.0	84	10.9	44	222
Chicken, stewing, dark meat without skin, stewed	4.1	95	15.3	53	258

POULTRY (continued)

Product (3½ ounces, cooked)	Saturated Fatty Acids (Grams)	Cholesterol (Milligrams)	Total Fat[1] (Grams)	Calories From Fat[2](%)	Total Calories
Duck, domesticated, flesh only, roasted	4.2	89	11.2	50	201
Chicken, broilers or fryers, dark meat with skin, roasted	4.4	91	15.8	56	253
Goose, domesticated, flesh only, roasted	4.6	96	12.7	48	238
Turkey bologna, about 3½ slices	5.1	99	15.2	69	199
Chicken frankfurter, about 2	5.5	101	19.5	68	257
Turkey frankfurter, about 2	5.9	107	17.7	70	226

FISH AND SHELLFISH

Omega-3 fatty acid (fish oil) is a type of polyunsaturated fat found in the greatest amounts in fattier fish. Evidence is mounting that omega-3 fatty acids in the diet may help lower high blood cholesterol. Since their potential benefit is not fully understood, the use of fish oil supplements is not recommended. However, eating fish is beneficial because it not only contains omega-3 fatty acids but, more important, it is low in saturated fat.

Product (3½ ounces, cooked)	Saturated Fatty Acids (Grams)	Cholesterol (Milligrams)	Omega-3 Fatty Acids (Grams)	Total Fat[1] (Grams)	Calories From Fat[2](%)	Total Calories
Finfish						
Haddock, dry heat	0.2	74	0.2	0.9	7	112
Cod, Atlantic, dry heat	0.2	55	0.2	0.9	7	105
Pollock, walleye, dry heat	0.2	96	1.5	1.1	9	113
Perch, mixed species, dry heat	0.2	42	0.3	1.2	9	117
Grouper, mixed species, dry heat	0.3	47	—	1.3	10	118

FISH AND SHELLFISH *(continued)*

Product (3½ ounces, cooked)	Saturated Fatty Acids (Grams)	Cholesterol (Milligrams)	Omega-3 Fatty Acids (Grams)	Total Fat[1] (Grams)	Calories From Fat[2](%)	Total Calories
Whiting, mixed species, dry heat	0.3	84	0.9	1.7	13	115
Snapper, mixed species, dry heat	0.4	47	—	1.7	12	128
Halibut, Atlantic and Pacific, dry heat	0.4	41	0.6	2.9	19	140
Rockfish, Pacific, dry heat	0.5	44	0.5	2.0	15	121
Sea bass, mixed species, dry heat	0.7	53	—	2.5	19	124
Trout, rainbow, dry heat	0.8	73	0.9	4.3	26	151
Swordfish, dry heat	1.4	50	1.1	5.1	30	155
Tuna, bluefin, dry heat	1.6	49	—	6.3	31	184
Salmon, sockeye, dry heat	1.9	87	1.3	11.0	46	216
Anchovy, European, canned	2.2	—	2.1	9.7	42	210
Herring, Atlantic, dry heat	2.6	77	2.1	11.5	51	203
Eel, dry heat	3.0	161	0.7	15.0	57	236
Mackerel, Atlantic, dry heat	4.2	75	1.3	17.8	61	262
Pompano, Florida, dry heat	4.5	64	—	12.1	52	211
Crustaceans						
Lobster, northern	0.1	72	0.1	0.6	6	98
Crab, blue, moist heat	0.2	100	0.5	1.8	16	102

FISH AND SHELLFISH (continued)

Product (3½ ounces, cooked)	Saturated Fatty Acids (Grams)	Cholesterol (Milligrams)	Omega-3 Fatty Acids (Grams)	Total Fat[1] (Grams)	Calories From Fat[2](%)	Total Calories
Shrimp, mixed species, moist heat	0.3	195	0.3	1.1	10	99
Mollusks						
Whelk, moist heat	0.1	130	—	0.8	3	275
Clam, mixed species, moist heat	0.2	67	0.3	2.0	12	148
Mussel, blue, moist heat	0.9	56	0.8	4.5	23	172
Oyster, Eastern, moist heat	1.3	109	1.0	5.0	33	137

DAIRY AND EGG PRODUCTS

Product	Saturated Fat (Grams)	Cholesterol (Milligrams)	Total Fat[1] (Grams)	Calories from Fat[2](%)	Total Calories
Milk (8 ounces)					
Skim milk	0.3	4	0.4	5	86
Buttermilk	1.3	9	2.2	20	99
Low-fat milk, 1% fat	1.6	10	2.6	23	102
Low-fat milk, 2% fat	2.9	18	4.7	35	121
Whole milk, 3.3% fat	5.1	33	8.2	49	150
Yogurt (4 ounces)					
Plain yogurt, low fat	0.1	2	0.2	3	63
Plain yogurt	2.4	14	3.7	47	70
Cheese					
Cottage cheese, low-fat, 1% fat, 4 oz.	0.7	5	1.2	13	82
Mozzarella, part-skim, 1 oz.	2.9	16	4.5	56	72
Cottage cheese, creamed, 4 oz.	3.2	17	5.1	39	117
Mozzarella, 1 oz.	3.7	22	6.1	69	80
Sour cream, 1 oz.	3.7	12	5.9	87	61

DAIRY AND EGG PRODUCTS *(continued)*

Product	Saturated Fat (Grams)	Cholesterol (Milligrams)	Total Fat[1] (Grams)	Calories from Fat[2](%)	Total Calories
American processed cheese spread, pasteurized, 1 oz.	3.8	16	6.0	66	82
Feta, 1 oz.	4.2	25	6.0	72	75
Neufchatel, 1 oz.	4.2	22	6.6	81	74
Camembert, 1 oz.	4.3	20	6.9	73	85
American processed cheese food, pasteurized, 1 oz.	4.4	18	7.0	68	93
Provolone, 1 oz.	4.8	20	7.6	68	100
Limburger, 1 oz.	4.8	26	7.7	75	93
Brie, 1 oz.	4.9	28	7.9	74	95
Romano, 1 oz.	4.9	29	7.6	63	110
Gouda, 1 oz.	5.0	32	7.8	69	101
Swiss, 1 oz.	5.0	26	7.8	65	107
Edam, 1 oz.	5.0	25	7.9	70	101
Brick, 1 oz.	5.3	27	8.4	72	105
Blue, 1 oz.	5.3	21	8.2	73	100
Gruyere, 1 oz.	5.4	31	9.2	71	117
Muenster, 1 oz.	5.4	27	8.5	74	104
Parmesan, 1 oz.	5.4	22	8.5	59	129
Monterey Jack, 1 oz.	5.5	25	8.6	73	106
Roquefort, 1 oz.	5.5	26	8.7	75	105
Ricotta, part-skim, 4 oz.	5.6	25	9.0	52	156
American processed cheese, pasteurized, 1 oz.	5.6	27	8.9	75	106
Colby, 1 oz.	5.7	27	9.1	73	112
Cheddar, 1 oz.	6.0	30	9.4	74	114
Cream cheese, 1 oz.	6.2	31	9.9	90	99
Ricotta, whole milk, 4 oz.	9.4	58	14.7	67	197
Eggs					
Egg, chicken, white	0	0	tr	0	16
Egg, chicken, whole	1.7	274	5.6	64	79
Egg, chicken, yolk	1.7	272	5.6	80	63

FROZEN DESSERTS

Product (1 cup)	Saturated Fatty Acids (Grams)	Cholesterol (Milligrams)	Total Fat[1] (Grams)	Calories from Fat[2](%)	Total Calories
Fruit Popsicle, 1 bar	—	—	0.0	0	65
Fruit ice	—	—	tr.	0	247
Fudgsicle	—	—	0.2	2	91
Frozen yogurt, fruit flavored	—	—	2.0	8	216
Sherbet, orange	2.4	14	3.8	13	270
Pudding pops, 1 pop	2.5	1	2.6	25	94
Ice milk, vanilla, soft serve	2.9	13	4.6	19	223
Ice milk, vanilla, hard	3.5	18	5.6	28	184
Ice cream, vanilla, regular	8.9	59	14.3	48	269
Ice cream, French vanilla, soft serve	13.5	153	22.5	54	377
Ice cream, vanilla, rich, 16% fat	14.7	88	23.7	61	349

FATS AND OILS

Product (1 tablespoon)	Saturated Fatty Acids (Grams)	Cholesterol (Milligrams)	Polyunsaturated Fatty Acids (Grams)	Monounsaturated Fatty Acids (Grams)
Rapeseed oil (canola oil)	0.9	0	4.5	7.6
Safflower oil	1.2	0	10.1	1.6
Sunflower oil	1.4	0	5.5	6.2
Peanut butter, smooth	1.5	0	2.3	3.7
Corn oil	1.7	0	8.0	3.3
Olive oil	1.8	0	1.1	9.9
Hydrogenated sun-flower oil	1.8	0	4.9	6.3
Margarine, liquid, bottled	1.8	0	5.1	3.9
Margarine, soft, tub	1.8	0	3.9	4.8
Sesame oil	1.9	0	5.7	5.4

FATS AND OILS (continued)

Product (1 tablespoon)	Saturated Fatty Acids (Grams)	Cholesterol (Milligrams)	Polyunsaturated Fatty Acids (Grams)	Monounsaturated Fatty Acids (Grams)
Soybean oil	2.0	0	7.9	3.2
Margarine, stick	2.1	0	3.6	5.1
Peanut oil	2.3	0	4.3	6.2
Cottonseed oil	3.5	0	7.1	2.4
Lard	5.0	12	1.4	5.8
Beef tallow	6.4	14	0.5	5.3
Palm oil	6.7	0	1.3	5.0
Butter	7.1	31	0.4	3.3
Cocoa butter	8.1	0	0.4	4.5
Palm kernel oil	11.1	0	0.2	1.5
Coconut oil	11.8	0	0.2	0.8

NUTS AND SEEDS

Product (1 ounce)	Saturated Fatty Acids (Grams)	Cholesterol (Milligrams)	Total Fat[1] (Grams)	Calories from Fat[2](%)	Total Calories
European chestnuts	0.2	0	1.1	9	105
Filberts or hazelnuts	1.3	0	17.8	89	179
Almonds	1.4	0	15.0	80	167
Pecans	1.5	0	18.4	89	187
Sunflower seed kernels, roasted	1.5	0	1.4	77	165
English walnuts	1.6	0	17.6	87	182
Pistachio nuts	1.7	0	13.7	75	164
Peanuts	1.9	0	14.0	76	164
Hickory nuts	2.0	0	18.3	88	187
Pine nuts, pignolia	2.2	0	14.4	89	146
Pumpkin and squash seed kernels	2.3	0	12.0	73	148
Cashew nuts	2.6	0	13.2	73	163
Macadamia nuts	3.1	0	20.9	95	199
Brazil nuts	4.6	0	18.8	91	186
Coconut meat, unsweetened	16.3	0	18.3	88	187

BREADS, CEREALS, PASTA, RICE, DRIED PEAS AND BEANS

Product	Saturated Fatty Acids (Grams)	Cholesterol (Milligrams)	Total Fat[1] (Grams)	Calories from Fat[2](%)	Total Calories
Breads					
Melba toast, 1 plain	0.1	0	tr.	0	20
Pita, ½ large shell	0.1	0	1.0	5	165
Corn tortilla	0.1	0	1.0	14	65
Rye bread, 1 slice	0.2	0	1.0	14	65
English muffin	0.3	0	1.0	6	140
Bagel, 1, 3½" diameter	0.3	0	2.0	9	200
White bread, 1 slice	0.3	0	1.0	14	65
Rye-Krisp, 2 triple crackers	0.3	0	1.0	16	56
Whole wheat bread, 1 slice	0.4	0	1.0	13	70
Saltines, 4	0.5	4	1.0	18	50
Hamburger bun	0.5	tr.	2.0	16	115
Hot dog bun	0.5	tr.	2.0	16	115
Pancake, 1, 4" diameter	0.5	16	2.0	30	60
Bran muffin, 1, 2½" diameter	1.4	24	6.0	43	125
Corn muffin, 1, 2½" diameter	1.5	23	5.0	31	145
Plain doughnut, 1, 3¼" diameter	2.8	20	12.0	51	210
Croissant, 1, 4½" by 4"	3.5	13	12.0	46	235
Waffle, 1, 7" diameter	4.0	102	13.0	48	245
Cereals (1 cup)					
Corn flakes	tr.	—	0.1	0	98
Cream of wheat, cooked	tr.	—	0.5	3	134
Corn grits, cooked	tr.	—	0.5	3	146
Oatmeal, cooked	0.4	—	2.4	15	145
Granola	5.8	—	33.1	50	595

BREADS, CEREALS, PASTA, RICE, DRIED PEAS AND BEANS *(continued)*

Product	Saturated Fatty Acids (Grams)	Cholesterol (Milligrams)	Total Fat[1] (Grams)	Calories from Fat[2](%)	Total Calories
100% natural cereal with raisins and dates	13.7	—	20.3	37	496
Pasta (1 cup)					
Spaghetti, cooked	0.1	0	1.0	6	155
Elbow macaroni, cooked	0.1	0	1.0	6	155
Egg noodles, cooked	0.5	50	2.0	11	160
Chow mein noodles, canned	2.1	5	11.0	45	220
Rice (1 cup cooked)					
Rice, white	0.1	0	0.5	2	225
Rice, brown	0.3	0	1.0	4	230
Dried Peas and Beans (1 cup cooked)					
Split peas	0.1	0	0.8	3	231
Kidney beans	0.1	0	1.0	4	225
Lima beans	0.2	0	0.7	3	217
Black-eyed peas	0.3	0	1.2	5	200
Garbanzo beans	0.4	0	4.3	14	269

SWEETS AND SNACKS

Product	Saturated Fatty Acids (Grams)	Cholesterol (Milligrams)	Total Fat[1] (Grams)	Calories from Fat[2](%)	Total Calories
Beverages					
Ginger ale, 12 oz.	0.0	0	0.0	0	125
Cola, regular, 12 oz.	0.0	0	0.0	0	160
Chocolate shake, 10 oz.	6.5	37	10.5	26	360
Candy (1 ounce)					
Hard candy	0.0	0	0.0	0	110

SWEETS AND SNACKS (continued)

Product	Saturated Fatty Acids (Grams)	Cholesterol (Milligrams)	Total Fat[1] (Grams)	Calories from Fat[2](%)	Total Calories
Gum drops	tr.	0	tr.	tr.	100
Fudge	2.1	1	3.0	24	115
Milk chocolate, plain	5.4	6	9.0	56	145
Cookies					
Vanilla wafers, 5 cookies, 1¾" diameter	0.9	12	3.3	32	94
Fig bars, 4 cookies 1⅝" × 1⅝" × ⅜"	1.0	27	4.0	17	210
Chocolate brownie with icing, 1½" by 1¾" by ⅞"	1.6	14	4.0	36	100
Oatmeal cookies, 4 cookies, 2⅝" diameter	2.5	2	10.0	37	245
Chocolate chip cookies, 4 cookies, 2¼" diameter	3.9	18	11.0	54	185
Cakes and Pies					
Angel food cake, 1/12 of 10" cake	tr	0	tr.	tr.	125
Gingerbread, 1/9 of 8" cake	1.1	1	4.0	21	175
White layer cake with white icing, 1/16 of 9" cake	2.1	3	9.0	32	260
Yellow layer cake with chocolate icing, 1/16 of 9" cake	3.0	36	8.0	31	235
Pound cake, 1/17 of loaf	3.0	64	5.0	41	110
Devil's food cake with chocolate icing, 1/16 of 9" cake	3.5	37	8.0	31	235
Lemon meringue pie, 1/6 of 9" pie	4.3	143	14.0	36	355

SWEETS AND SNACKS *(continued)*

Product	Saturated Fatty Acids (Grams)	Cholesterol (Milligrams)	Total Fat[1] (Grams)	Calories from Fat[2](%)	Total Calories
Apple pie, ⅙ of 9″ pie	4.6	0	18.0	40	405
Cream pie, ⅙ of 9″ pie	15.0	8	23.0	46	455
Snacks					
Popcorn, air-popped, 1 cup	tr.	0	tr.	tr.	30
Pretzels, stick, 2¼″, 10 pretzels	tr.	0	tr.	tr.	10
Popcorn with oil and salted, 1 cup	0.5	0	3.0	49	55
Corn chips, 1 oz.	1.4	25	9.0	52	155
Potato chips, 1 oz.	2.6	0	10.1	62	147
Pudding					
Gelatin	0.0	0	0.0	0	70
Tapioca, ½ cup	2.3	15	4.0	25	145
Chocolate pudding, ½ cup	2.4	15	4.0	24	150

MISCELLANEOUS

Product	Saturated Fatty Acids (Grams)	Cholesterol (Milligrams)	Total Fat[1] (Grams)	Calories from Fat[2](%)	Total Calories
Gravies (½ cup)					
Au jus, canned	0.1	1	0.3	3	80
Turkey, canned	0.7	3	2.5	37	61
Beef, canned	1.4	4	2.8	41	62
Chicken, canned	1.7	3	6.8	65	95
Sauces (½ cup)					
Sweet and sour	tr.	0	0.1	<1	147
Barbecue	0.3	0	2.3	22	94

MISCELLANEOUS (continued)

Product	Saturated Fatty Acids (Grams)	Cholesterol (Milligrams)	Total Fat[1] (Grams)	Calories from Fat[2](%)	Total Calories
White	3.2	17	6.7	50	121
Cheese	4.7	26	8.6	50	154
Sour cream	8.5	45	15.1	53	255
Hollandaise	20.9	94	34.1	87	353
Bearnaise	20.9	99	34.1	88	351
Salad dressings (1 tablespoon)					
Russian, low calorie	0.1	1	0.7	27	23
French, low calorie	0.1	1	0.9	37	22
Italian, low calorie	0.2	1	1.5	85	16
Thousand Island, low calorie	0.2	2	1.6	59	24
Imitation mayonnaise	0.5	4	2.9	75	35
Thousand Island, regular	0.9	—	5.6	86	59
Italian, regular	1.0	—	7.1	93	69
Russian, regular	1.1	—	7.8	92	76
French, regular	1.5	—	6.4	86	67
Blue cheese	1.5	—	8.0	93	77
Mayonnaise	1.6	8	11.0	100	99
Other					
Olives, green, 4 medium	0.2	0	1.5	90	15
Nondairy creamer, powdered, 1 teaspoon	0.7	0	1.0	90	10
Avocado, Florida	5.3	0	27.0	72	340
Pizza, cheese, ⅛ of 15" diameter	4.1	56	9.0	28	290
Quiche lorraine, ⅛ of 8" diameter	23.2	285	48.0	72	600

[1]Total fat = saturated fatty acids plus monounsaturated fatty acids plus polyunsaturated fatty acids.
[2]Percent calories from fat = (total fat calories divided by total calories) multiplied by 100; total fat calories = fat (grams) multiplied by 9.
— = Information not available in the sources used.
Adapted from "Eating to Lower Your High Blood Cholesterol," National Heart, Lung and Blood Institute, Bethesda, Maryland.

Cardiac Glossary

Acute Having a rapid, intense onset and usually a short course with severe symptoms.

ACE inhibitors A new class of drugs that lower blood pressure by interfering with the body's production of angiotensin.

Adrenaline (epinephrine) One of the hormones produced by the adrenal glands. It narrows the small blood vessels, increases the heart rate, and raises the blood pressure.

Aerobic exercise A method of physical exercise for producing beneficial changes in the respiratory and circulatory systems by activities that require only a modest increase in oxygen intake.

Ambulatory EKG monitoring See *Holter monitor* below.

Amphetamines A class of drugs which stimulate the nervous system and suppress appetite.

Anaerobic exercise A method of physical exercise in which more oxygen is used than is available, leading to exhaustion.

Aneurysm A ballooning-out of the wall of a heart chamber or a blood vessel due to a weakening of the wall by disease, injury, or congenital defect.

Angina (angina pectoris) Discomfort in the chest or at other locations (back, arm, neck, etc.) due to inadequate supply of blood and oxygen to the heart muscle, resulting from the narrowing of one or more coronary arteries.

Angiogram Pictures of heart chambers or blood vessels taken during the course of angiography examination. See *angiography*, below.

Angiography An X-ray technique that involves the injection of dye into the heart chambers or blood vessels, through a catheter, resulting in a detailed picture of the inside of these structures. See *angiogram*, above.

Angioplasty A surgical technique using a "balloon catheter" to dilate arteries at the point where they have become narrowed by a *plaque* (see below).

Angiotensin converting enzyme inhibitors. See *ACE inhibitors*, above.

Antianginal A drug used to relieve angina symptoms.

Antiarrhythmic A drug that helps control or prevent cardiac arrhythmias.

Anticoagulant Commonly called "blood thinners," these are drugs that retard the blood-clotting process.

Antihypertensive A drug that lowers blood pressure.

Aorta The body's largest artery, it carries blood from the main pumping chamber (left ventricle) of the heart and distributes it to all parts of the body.

Aortic valve The valve through which oxygenated blood passes from the main pumping chamber (left ventricle) of the heart to the body's largest artery (aorta).

Arrhythmia Any disturbance of the heart's normal rhythm.

Arterioles The smallest arteries of the body, these conduct blood to the capillaries.

Arteriosclerosis (commonly called "hardening of the arteries") A disease of the lining of a coronary artery which results in hardening and loss of elasticity of the arterial walls.

Arteriosclerotic heart disease See *ischemic heart disease,* below.

Artery A blood vessel that transports blood away from the heart to the rest of the body. An artery usually carries oxygenated blood, except for the pulmonary artery, which carries unoxygenated blood from the heart to the lungs for a new oxygen supply.

Atheroma A mass of yellowish fatty and cellular material that forms in and behind the inner lining of arterial walls.

Atherosclerosis A form of arteriosclerosis in which, in addition to the hardening and loss of elasticity of the arteries, a fatty substance (plaque) forms on the inner walls of the arteries, frequently causing obstruction to the flow of blood. See *arteriosclerosis,* above.

Atrium One of the two upper chambers of the heart that receive unoxygenated blood from the body or lungs and transports it to the ventricles.

Atroventricular node A small nodule of muscular fibers at the base of the wall behind the right and left atria, which conducts impulses from the sinoatrial node to the ventricle.

Auscultation The act of listening to sounds within the body, usually with a stethoscope.

Beta-blocker A drug that blocks the action of the beta receptors, the nerve endings that affect the heart rate and force of contraction. Such drugs are used for the treatment and control of angina, high blood pressure, and certain cardiac arrhythmias.

Bile acid sequestrants These medications (e.g., cholestyramine, colestipol) bind cholesterol-containing bile acids in the intestines and remove them in the feces.

Blood pressure The force exerted by the blood against the arterial walls, created by the heart as it pumps blood to all parts of the body.

Blood vessel A vein or artery.

Brachycardia An abnormally slow heart rate, usually less than 60 beats per minute.

Bypass surgery See *coronary artery bypass surgery*, below.

Calcium channel blocker A drug that blocks the calcium transport mechanism in blood vessels and heart muscle cells. Such drugs relax the walls of the coronary arteries, preventing coronary spasm. They are used mainly for the treatment and prevention of angina.

Calorie A numerical unit used to express the amount of heat output of an organism and the fuel or energy value of food.

Capillaries Tiny, thin-walled blood vessels forming a network between the arterioles and the veins, these facilitate the exchange of substances between the surrounding tissues and the blood.

Carbohydrate One of the three food ingredients that supply energy to the body and are essential for normal body function.

Cardiac Pertaining to the heart.

Cardiac arrest Abrupt cessation of heartbeat.

Cardiac catheterization See *catheterization*, below.

Cardiac cycle One complete heartbeat, consisting of a contraction and a relaxation of the heart.

Cardiac output The amount of blood pumped by the heart each minute.

Cardiologist A physician specializing in the diagnosis and treatment of heart disease.

Cardiology The study of the heart in health and disease.

Cardiomyopathy A term for diseases of the heart muscle (myocardium) which can cause it to become stiff and weak.

Cardiopulmonary Pertaining to the heart and lungs.

Cardiopulmonary resuscitation (CPR) Emergency procedure for reviving heart and lung function, using special physical techniques and electrical and mechanical equipment.

Cardiovascular Pertaining to the heart and blood vessels.

Cardioversion The restoration of normal heart rhythm in patients afflicted with certain cardiac arrhythmias, using an electric shock applied across the chest wall.

Catheter A thin, flexible tube that can be guided through a vein or artery (in the groin or arm) into the heart. It can be used to measure pressures, inject X-ray dye, or open up arteries.

Catheterization In cardiology, the process of introducing a catheter into a vein or artery, then directing it toward the heart.

Cholesterol A natural body fat found in foods of animal origin (meat, dairy products), but not in foods of plant origin; an ingredient in fatty plaques that may block coronary arteries. Blood cholesterol is made up of cholesterol manufactured in the liver and absorbed from ingested food.

Chronic Of long duration or frequent recurrence.

Circulatory Pertaining to the heart, blood vessels, and circulation.

Coagulation The formation of a clot.

Collateral circulation Circulation pathways using nearby smaller vessels going around a main artery that has been blocked.

Complex carbohydrates Starch and fiber sugars from plants.

Congenital Pertaining to an inherited feature; that which is present at birth.

Congestive heart failure A condition in which a weakened heart is unable to pump enough blood, effectively leading to congestion of the lungs and retention of water in the body.

Constriction The act of being narrowed or tightened by an inward pressure.

Contrast agent An organic iodine solution that increases the radiodensity of blood so that the blood vessels will contrast with soft tissues of the heart and/or other tissues.

Coronary Pertaining to the coronary arteries, the blood vessels that supply the heart muscle with blood and oxygen. Also, used as a noun, an abbreviated term for heart attack.

Coronary arteries See *coronary*, above.

Coronary arteriogram Pictures of coronary arteries taken with an X-ray technique involving injection of dye into the heart's blood vessels. See *angiography*, above.

Coronary artery bypass surgery The surgical revascularization (see below) of the heart, using healthy blood vessels of the patient to bypass or circumvent obstructed coronary arteries and improve blood flow.

Coronary artery disease Atherosclerosis of the coronary arteries. See *atherosclerosis*, above.

Coronary artery risk factor See *risk factor*, below.

Coronary thrombosis A blood clot in the coronary artery.

CT scan In cardiology, a computer X-ray technique (computer tomography) for heart scanning.

Cyanosis A bluish discoloration of the skin, fingernails, and lips, due to insufficient amount of oxygen in the blood. It is seen in patients with certain types of congenital heart defects and other diseases.

Defibrillation Termination of fibrillation (see below). Usually refers to the treatment of atrial or ventricular fibrillation (a life-threatening arrhythmia) by the application of an electric shock (cardioversion) and/or drugs.

Diabetes mellitus A disorder of sugar metabolism characterized by inadequate production or utilization of the hormone insulin.

Diastole The period of each heartbeat during which the pumping chambers (ventricles) relax and fill with blood.

Diastolic blood pressure The diastolic reading obtained in blood pressure measurement, i.e., the second and lower number.

Dietary cholesterol Cholesterol contained in ingested foods.

Digitalis A drug that strengthens the force of contraction of the heart and slows the rate at which it beats. Digitalis drugs are used in the treatment of congestive heart failure and in the management of certain cardiac arrhythmias.

Dilatation Enlargement of the blood vessels (usually arteries) or heart chambers.

Diuretic A drug that increases the flow of urine and excretion of body fluid.

Dyspnea Difficulty in breathing.

Echocardiography A diagnostic technique that uses ultrasound waves to visualize and examine the heart structures. The pictorial record is called an *echocardiogram*.

Edema Swelling of body tissue caused by a buildup of fluid.

Effusion Accumulation of fluid between body tissues or in organs.

Ejection fraction A measurement of left ventricular contraction that provides a useful measure of left ventricular function.

Electrocardiography A diagnostic technique in which small electrodes are placed on the patient's chest, arms, and legs for the purpose of recording the electrical activity of the heart. The resulting tracing is called an electrocardiogram (EKG or ECG).

EKG Electrocardiogram; a record of the electrical activity of the heart (sometimes called ECG).

Embolism The blocking of a blood vessel by a clot (embolus) carried in the bloodstream from another location where it is formed.

Embolus A bit of matter (generally a blood clot) that drifts unattached in the bloodstream until it lodges in a blood vessel and obstructs it.

Endocarditis Infection of the inner lining of the heart chambers (endocardium).

Endothelium The single layer of smooth, thin cells that lines the heart, blood vessels, lymph vessels, and body cavities.

Epinephrine A hormone secreted by the adrenal gland upon stimulation of the sympathetic nervous system in response to stress such as anger or fear. Produces increase in heart rate, blood pressure, cardiac output, and sugar metabolism.

EPS Electrophysiological study. An invasive method for study of the basic electrical activity of the heart. Used in patients with serious arrhythmia.

Exercise echocardiogram An echocardiographic study performed during and after exercise. Correlated with a simultaneously performed electrocardiographic stress test. See *echocardiogram*, above.

Exercise stress test A test that symptomatically and electrocardiographically measures the heart's ability to tolerate an increased rate. See *stress test*, below.

Extrasystole A premature beat, originating in either a ventricle or atrium. See *ventricular premature beat*, below.

Fat A component of most foods of plant or animal origin. An essential element in the diet.

Fatty acids The basic chemical units of fats. These can be either saturated, monounsaturated, or polyunsaturated, depending on how many hydrogen atoms they hold. All dietary fats are a mixture of the three types of fatty acids in varying amounts.

Fiber A nondigestible type of complex carbohydrate.

Fibrillation Uncoordinated contraction of the heart muscle. It may involve the upper chambers (atrial fibrillation) or the lower chambers (ventricular fibrillation). See *ventricular fibrillation*, below.

Framingham Heart Study An epidemiological heart study performed in a town in eastern Massachusetts since 1948, the source of well over 400 scientific publications regarding the natural life histories and the specifics of all aspects of cardiovascular disease including risk factors, hypertension, etc.

HDL See *high-density lipoproteins*, below.

Heart attack See *myocardial infarction*, below.

Heart block An arrhythmia caused by disruption (either partial or total) of the heart's electrical conduction pathways.

Heart failure See *congestive heart failure*, above.

Heart-lung machine A machine through which the bloodstream is diverted for pumping and oxygenation during heart surgery.

Heart murmur An abnormal sound that can be heard through the chest with a stethoscope, resulting from turbulence in the bloodstream. It generally represents a malfunctioning heart valve.

Hemorrhage Abnormal bleeding and loss of blood.

High blood pressure See *hypertension*, below.

High-density lipoproteins (HDL) Lipoproteins that contain a small amount of cholesterol and that help to carry cholesterol away from body cells. The higher the HDL level, the better, as far as arteriosclerosis is concerned.

Holter monitor A portable electrocardiograph worn by a patient over an extended period, to assess the effects of activities of daily living on the electrocardiogram.

Hormone Glandular secretion transported by the bloodstream to various organs in order to regulate vital functions and processes.

Hydrogenation The chemical process that changes liquid vegetable oils (unsaturated fats) to a more solid (saturated) form.

Hypercholesterolemia An excess of cholesterol in the blood.

Hypertension High blood pressure. A condition characterized by excessive pressure within the arteries.

Hypertrophic cardiomyopathy Enlargement of the left ventricle of the heart, resulting from a heart disease of unknown cause (possibly congenital). May cause congestive heart failure or sudden death.

Hypertrophy Increased size and thickening of a muscle, thereby strengthening the force of contraction. It commonly occurs in the heart.

Hypotension Low blood pressure.

Infarction An irreversible injury to an area of the heart, usually as a result of a total blockage of the blood supply to the region. See *myocardial infarction*, below.

Insufficiency See *regurgitation*, below.

Intravenous Within a vein. A route for administration of drugs and other products.

Invasive procedure A procedure that requires the entry of a needle, catheter, or other instrument into the body.

Ischemia A local, usually temporary, deficiency in oxygen supply to an organ or tissue due to obstruction or narrowing of the artery supplying that part. See also *myocardial ischemia*, below.

Ischemic heart disease Heart disease most commonly resulting from atherosclerotic narrowing or obstruction of the coronary arteries.

Kidneys The organs that regulate salt and water metabolism and remove waste products from the bloodstream into the urine.

Lesion An abnormal structural defect, such as the narrowing of a coronary artery seen at surgery or on an angiogram.

LDL See *low-density lipoproteins*, below.

Lipid Fat or fatlike substance; examples are cholesterol and triglycerides.

Lipoprotein A blood compound consisting of lipid (fat) and protein molecules bound together. Lipoproteins carry fat and cholesterol through the bloodstream.

Low-density lipoproteins (LDL) Lipoproteins that carry the largest amount of cholesterol in the blood. LDL is responsible for depositing cholesterol in the artery walls.

Lumen The canal, duct, or cavity of a tubular organ.

Lungs Two spongelike organs that oxygenate the blood and expel gaseous waste (carbon dioxide) from the body.

Marfan's syndrome An inherited disease characterized by a generalized abnormality of the connective tissues of the body. It may have major effects on the heart, blood vessels, and skeletal and ocular systems.

Milligram (mg) A unit of weight equal to one thousandth of a gram. There are 28,350 mg in one ounce.

Milligram/deciliter (mg/dl) A method of expressing concentration of solids in liquids. In blood cholesterol measurements, the weight of cholesterol (in milligrams) in a deciliter (about 1/10 of a quart) of blood.

Mitral valve A heart valve through which blood passes from the left upper chamber (left atrium) to the main pumping chamber (left ventricle).

Mitral valve prolapse A condition in which the mitral valve prolapses and the edges of the valve leaflets do not come together properly.

Monounsaturated fat A class of fats that lack a hydrogen band in one point in the carbon chain; tends to be associated with lower blood cholesterol content.

MRI Magnetic resonance imaging, a non X-ray method which can be used to study the heart and other organs.

Murmur See *heart murmur,* above.

Myocardial infarction An irreversible injury to an area of heart muscle caused by blockage of a coronary artery. See *infarction,* above.

Myocardial ischemia Ischemia of the heart muscle. See *ischemia,* above.

Myocardium The heart muscle.

Negative In medicine, means normal or showing the absence of disease.

Niacin B vitamin essential for cellular energy production. In large doses, a cholesterol-lowering agent.

Nicotine A powerful addictive drug which is the most dangerous component in cigarette smoke.

Nicotine gum Brand name is Nicorette. The first drug which has proven effective in replacing the physiological effects of nicotine. Helps in quitting cigarette smoking.

Nitrates Drugs that relax the walls of blood vessels, especially arteries, causing them to dilate. Used mainly in the management of angina. See *nitroglycerine,* below.

Nitroglycerin A drug that relaxes the walls of blood vessels, causing them to dilate. Used primarily for the treatment of angina attacks.

Noninvasive procedure A medical procedure or test that does not require entry of a needle, catheter, or instrument into the body.

Nuclear cardiology That area of cardiology which uses radioactive substances in heart studies.

Obesity An excess of body fat. Should be distinguished from heaviness (body weight). Generally defined as at least 10–20 percent excess over "ideal" body weight (based on one's age, height, and bone structure).

Occlusion Total closure of a blood vessel.

Open-heart surgery Surgery performed on the heart, its chambers, and/or the coronary arteries while the patient's blood is diverted through a heart-lung machine.

Orthopnea A condition in which one has difficulty in breathing except when sitting or standing upright.

Outpatient procedure A test or procedure performed outside of a hospital.

Oxygen A gas that is essential for life and that is necessary for energy-producing chemical reactions in the cells of the body. Extracted from air inhaled into the lungs, it enters the bloodstream and is carried by the blood to the body tissues.

Pacemaker A natural mechanism that generates tiny electrical impulses, setting the pace for the heartbeat. Artificial pacemakers are electronic devices that can be implanted under the skin and that act as a substitute for a defective natural pacemaker. See *sinoatrial node*, below.

Palpitations An unpleasant awareness of the heartbeat. Often described as skipped, fluttering, forceful, and/or irregular heart activity.

Pericarditis Inflammation of the pericardium (see below).

Pericardium A thin membrane sac that surrounds the heart.

PET test Positron-emission tomography. A heart test using special radionuclides.

Physiology The science that studies the functions of body organs.

Plaque Abnormal buildup of fatty deposits on the inner layer of an artery. Plaques reduce the internal diameter of the artery, and may lead to total blockage. See *atheroma*, above.

Platelets Tiny cells of the blood that play an important part in the blood-clotting mechanism.

Platelet inhibitors Drugs which inhibit blood clot formation. Common examples are aspirin and Persantine.

Polyunsaturated fats Fats so constituted chemically that they are capable of absorbing additional atoms of hydrogen. They are predominantly vegetable in origin, contain no cholesterol, and are usually liquid at room temperature.

Positive In medicine, means abnormal or showing the presence of disease.

Potassium An essential mineral that is necessary for muscle contraction.

Prognosis Prediction or forecast of the probable course of a disease.

Prophylaxis Prevention of disease. For example, in cardiology, the use of antibiotics to prevent an infection of the heart valves.

Protein One of the three nutrients that supply calories to the body.

PTCA Percutaneous transluminal coronary angioplasty. See *angioplasty,* above.

Pulmonary Pertaining to the lungs.

Pulmonary artery The large artery that transports unoxygenated blood from the right ventricle to the lungs. This is the only artery in the body that carries unoxygenated blood.

Pulmonary circulation The circulation that carries unoxygenated blood from the heart to the lungs. It includes the right heart chambers, the main pulmonary artery, and the smaller pulmonary arteries.

Pulmonary edema A severe form of congestive heart failure in which flooding of fluid into the air sacs in the lungs occurs, producing severe shortness of breath.

Pulmonary embolism A condition in which a blood clot (embolus) has become dislodged, travels through the bloodstream and becomes lodged in one of the arteries in the lungs.

Pulmonic valve A heart valve through which unoxygenated blood passes from the right ventricle into the pulmonary artery, and is then transported to the lungs.

Pulse The expansion and contraction of an artery, which may be felt with the fingers.

QRS complex Part of an electrocardiographic tracing.

Radioisotope A radioactive material used in medical testing as well as in physical and biological research. Examples are thallium 201 and technetium 99m.

Radionuclide A radioactive material. See *radioisotope,* above.

Rales Moist, crackling sounds that can be heard over the lower portion of the lungs, virtually always present in patients with congestive heart failure.

Regurgitation (or insufficiency) The backward leakage of blood through a defective valve.

Renal Pertaining to the kidneys.

Respiration The act of breathing, inhalation and exhalation of air.

Resuscitation Restoration of breathing and heartbeat.

Revascularization To improve the blood circulation, surgically or by other means.

Risk factor A lifestyle habit, trait, condition, illness, or physical finding associated with increased risk or likelihood of a disease, such as coronary artery heart disease.

SALP The signal-averaged late potential EKG, a new computerized EKG.

Saturated fats Fats so constituted chemically that they are not capable of absorbing additional atoms of hydrogen. They are predominantly of animal origin (meat, milk), and are usually solid at room temperature.

Septum A dividing wall between two chambers. The ventricular septum is located between the two ventricles; the atrial septum is located between the two atria.

Serum The clear pale-yellow liquid that separates from the clot after blood coagulates. The liquid portion of blood that carries nutrients and other substances to and from the tissues.

Shock A condition resulting from inadequate circulation. It may be due to loss of blood or to extreme weakness of the heart as a pump. Shock is marked by low blood pressure, rapid pulse, paleness, and cold, clammy skin.

Shunt Diversion of blood between the two sides of the heart, owing to the presence of an abnormal opening within or near the heart. Shunts may also occur between two vessels distant from the heart.

Silent heart disease Symptom-free heart disorders, including ischemia, heart attacks, and even sudden death. See *silent myocardial ischemia*, below.

Silent myocardial ischemia Symptom-free ischemia or inadequate coronary artery blood flow. See *silent heart disease*, above.

Sinoatrial node The natural pacemaker of the heart. A small bundle of specialized cells that generates tiny electrical impulses that spread from the upper to the lower heart chambers, setting the pace of the heartbeat.

Sinus rhythm Normal heart rhythm that occurs because of the electrical impulses initiated in the sinoatrial node.

Sodium An essential mineral that is necessary to keep fluids distributed in the body. Table salt (sodium chloride) is nearly half sodium.

Spasm Temporary contraction of a muscular segment. Occurs in arterial walls, usually making the lumen smaller. See *vasoconstriction* and *vasospasm*, below.

Sphygmomanometer An instrument used to measure blood pressure.

Stenosis Narrowing or stricture of an opening, blood vessel, or valve.

Stethoscope A listening instrument that amplifies sounds within the body.

Stress test A test of cardiovascular health conducted by recording heart rate, blood pressure, electrocardiogram, and other measurements while a person undergoes physical exertion or drug induced stress. See *exercise stress test*, above.

Stroke Damage to the brain caused by an interruption of the blood flow to the brain.

Sudden cardiac death Totally unexpected death occurring within one hour of the onset of symptoms in a victim with or without known, preexisting heart disease.

Syncope A fainting spell. A sudden loss of consciousness owing to a temporary reduction of blood flow and oxygen supply to the brain.

Systemic circulation The general circulation, as opposed to the pulmonary circulation. It carries oxygenated blood to the entire body (except the lungs).

Systole The period of each heartbeat during which the pumping chambers contract and eject their blood content. The systolic reading obtained in blood pressure measurement is the first and higher number.

Systolic blood pressure The maximum arterial blood pressure which occurs at the end of the left ventricle's contraction.

Tachycardia An abnormally fast heart rate. Generally, anything over 100 beats per minute is considered tachycardia.

Thallium stress test A stress test conducted by injecting a small amount of radioactive substance (thallium) into the bloodstream and measuring its passage through the heart. See *stress test*, above.

Thrombolysis Lysis (or dissolving) of a clot or thrombus, usually by drugs known as *thrombolytic agents*. See *TPA*, below.

Thrombosis The formation of a blood clot (thrombus) that partially or completely blocks a blood vessel.

Total fat The sum of saturated, monounsaturated, and polyunsaturated fats present in the diet.

TPA (tissue plasminogen activator) A clot-dissolving enzyme occurring naturally in small amounts in the blood, but now produced in large amounts by genetic engineering techniques.

Treadmill test A stress test performed by using a motorized treadmill to produce physical stress. See *stress test*, above.

Tricuspid valve The heart valve through which blood passes from the right atrium to the right ventricle.

Triglyceride A common type of lipid (fat) carried in the bloodstream and found in fatty tissue, primarily ingested with fat in the diet.

Unsaturated fats See *monounsaturated fats* and *polyunsaturated fats*, above.

Valve A flexible structure that regulates the flow of blood within the heart. It allows the blood to circulate in only one direction, and prevents it from backing up.

Vascular Pertaining to blood vessels.

Vascular disease An ailment of the blood vessels often caused by atherosclerosis; may occur anywhere in the body (brain, legs, coronary arteries, etc.).

Vasoconstriction Narrowing of blood vessels produced by contraction of the muscles in their walls. See *vasospasm*, below.

Vasodilator A drug that lowers blood pressure by relaxing the muscular walls of arteries causing them to dilate.

Vasospasm Constriction or narrowing of an artery, leading to a decrease in its diameter and in the amount of blood it can deliver. See *vasoconstriction*, above.

Vein Any of the blood vessels that carry unoxygenated blood from all parts of the body back to the heart.

Ventricle One of the two pumping lower chambers of the heart. The left ventricle pumps oxygenated blood through the arteries to all parts of the body except the lungs. The right ventricle pumps unoxygenated blood through the pulmonary artery to the lungs.

Ventricular contraction Contraction of the left and/or right ventricles, the major chambers of the heart.

Ventricular fibrillation A heart arrhythmia characterized by rapid, chaotic electrical impulses, resulting in ineffectual contraction of the ventricles and loss of pulse and blood pressure. If it continues, death ensues.

Ventricular premature beats Premature beats or contractions originating in a ventricle.

Ventricular relaxation The phase of the heart cycle in which the ventricles are relaxed and filling with blood.

Ventriculogram An X-ray or radionuclide picture of the major chambers of the heart.

Very low density lipoproteins A class of lipoprotein that transports cholesterol and triglycerides in the bloodstream.

Index